Parenting Moral Teens in Immoral Times

Parenting Moral Teens in Immoral Times

edited by
Ron Brusius

Publishing House
St. Louis

Unless otherwise stated, the Scripture quotations in this publication are from The Holy Bible: NEW INTERNATIONAL VERSION, copyright © 1973, 1978, 1984 by the International Bible Society. Used by permission of Zondervan Bible Publishers.

Copyright © 1989 by Concordia Publishing House
3558 S. Jefferson Ave., St. Louis, MO 63118-3968
Manufactured in the United States of America

All rights reserved. No part of this publication may be reproduced, stored in a retrieval system, or transmitted, in any form or by any means, electronic, mechanical, photocopying, recording, or otherwise, without the prior written permission of Concordia Publishing House.

Library of Congress Cataloging-in-Publication Data

Parenting moral teens in immoral times
Ron Brusius, editor.
p. cm.
ISBN 0-570-04521-5
1. Family—Religious life. 2. Teenagers—Religious life. 3. Parenting—Religious aspects—Christianity. I. Brusius, Ron, 1934-
BV4526.2.P35 1989
248.8′4—dc19   88-26041
                                                                                        CIP

---

1 2 3 4 5 6 7 8 9 10   98 97 96 95 94 93 92 91 90 89

Contents

Preface Ron Brusius	6
"Oh, Lord, What Do I Say? (Talking to Teens about Sex) Bill Ameiss	8

The Three R's of Teen Sexuality
    (Talking to Teens about Teen Pregnancy)
    Jean Garton
	25

Sexual Identity: Who Sets the Agenda
    (Talking to Teens about Homosexuality)
    Ron Brusius
	39

No Uncertain Trumpets (Talking to Teens about Suicide) Bob Morrison	54

Healthy Sexuality vs. "Safe" Sex
    (Talking to Teens about AIDS and STD)
    Howard Mueller
	67

My Kid on Drugs—Never!
    (Talking to Teens about Drug and Alcohol Addiction
    Ed Eggert
	81

Violence and Victims: Making Nobody's Day
    (Talking to Teens about Violence)
    Betty Brusius
	96

"Turn That Thing Down!!!"
    (Talking to Teens about Rock Music)
    Annette Frank
	111

Counterfeit Religions in The Light
    (Talking to Teens about Cults)
    Bruce Frederickson
	127

"Tho' Devils All the World Should Fill. . ."
    (Talking to Teens about the Occult)
    Bruce Frederickson
	144

Peacemaking on the Family Front Jan Case	160

Preface

Social issues constantly confront us as Christian parents. We are always looking for satisfactory ways to deal with those issues ourselves. We also want to pass on our values and our perceptions to our teens. The 10 issues addressed in this book are issues which haunt—and even divide—our society today as we struggle for answers to the dilemmas they represent. They are presented here in a Christian frame of reference and offered to parents who seek information and suggestions on how to talk to their teens.

Several issues come up repeatedly. For example, rock music is discussed from several different perspectives. The emphasis given to rock music highlights the dilemma which faces us as we recognize rock as the music of choice for many Christian young people. At the same time we must acknowledge the destructive influences which some of the songs represent and promote.

A world corrupted by sin, the common human predicament affecting every age since the Fall, has always threatened society's existence by attacking its value system. A pervading belief in God, however distorted that may have been at times, has until recently held society together and reinforced innate moral values. During the past two and a half centuries, the erosion of Christian beliefs, the *overemphasis* on human potential, an obsessive drive for independence and freedom, among other factors—all converging at a time of almost instantaneous communication and transportation—have created a value-free society that has, in effect, declared there is no God. Volumes have been written on this subject, though only a few, such as Herbert Schlossberg in *Idols for Destruction*, have been sufficiently discerning and understanding of the Biblical connection and implications.

While this sordid yet fascinating story is itself a complex topic too detailed for study here, it must be the backdrop for this book. Otherwise the recommendations and suggestions offered here are mere Band-Aid treatments that will produce no lasting results. All of the authors approach their topics with the above understanding, whether or not they have had sufficient space here to articulate the cause-and-effect relationship in specific Biblical terms.

Each contributor has many qualifications for writing on the particular topic. Bill Ameiss is a youth executive, author, and lecturer. Jean Garton is a special consultant to the president of The Lutheran Church—Missouri Synod. Bob Morrison heads The Lutheran Church—Missouri Synod Office of Government Information in Washington, D.C. Howard Mueller is a former hospital chaplain now with The Lutheran Church–Missouri Synod Board for Social Ministry Services. Ed Eggert is a hospital chaplain in the field of chemical dependency. Betty Brusius is the executive director of the National Lutheran Parent-Teacher League. Annette Frank is a teacher and free-lance writer. Bruce Frederickson is a high school teacher and author. Jan Case is a parish pastor and family-life specialist.

Ron Brusius, Director
Adult and Family Life
The Lutheran Church—Missouri Synod

O Lord, What Do I Say?

Bill Ameiss

I know I should say something to my kids about sex! But I'm not sure what to say! If I ask them 'How's it going?' I'm afraid they'll think I assume they're up to something!"

"What I'm worried about is what if my kids are 'up to something'? I don't think I'd know how to deal with it. I've told them what's right and wrong! They're basically good, Christian kids, but somehow they see this whole business of sex differently than we do. I just don't seem to be able to get anywhere with them. They write me off as old fashioned."

"Well, what I worry about is their reaction! I mean, if I say a lot about sex, that opens up the whole subject. I don't believe they think of their father and me as . . . well . . . sexual. They know we share the same bedroom, but I don't think they always make the connection. To talk a lot about sexual issues gets awfully close to talking about me . . . and my experience. I'm not sure they're ready for that! I'm not so sure I'm ready for that."

"Frankly I'm not sure we ought to say a whole lot of anything to our teens. Look at all they're exposed to on TV and in the magazines! They get the impression that everything is sex, sex, sex. There's a lot more to life than sex, and they need to learn that!"

"Well, as far as I'm concerned, that's the reason for saying something. Everything is sex, sex, sex! And what they're seeing isn't good sex, let alone a Christian view of sex. I think we need to talk with them. I think they need to know the values we hold as Christian parents. I'm afraid they don't always hear those. I know they don't hear Christian values out there in the world. I just don't think we have any choice!"

"I think I agree with you. If kids are to get a healthy Christian view of sex, it has to come from us. I don't think they have a chance at developing Christian values about sex. If we don't teach a solid Christian understanding of sex in our homes, schools and churches, the kids won't stand a chance, and we have only ourselves to blame!"

Sound familiar? Have you been part of a conversation like the one above? Do any of these thoughts echo some of your own? Chances are, if you are like most parents, you have thought or spoken aloud most if not all of these comments! They reflect our concerns and our fears. We struggle with every possible feeling and every possible issue. We think it through from every possible angle and sometimes we're still stumped! We experience every possible emotion. It's that kind of issue. It's an explosive issue. What should we say to our kids? What shouldn't we say to our kids?

This chapter answers the question, "Should we talk to our kids about sexual issues?" with an emphatic "Yes, of course we should!" And if it were just that simple, this chapter could be about three pages long!

To Decide Means to Face Other Decisions

To decide to talk to your teens about sex is a good decision. It's, frankly, the only possible decision for a parent who wishes to be fully responsible as a Christian man or woman. But once that decision is made, a whole list of other questions pop up, waiting for answers! What should teens be told? Who should tell them? How detailed should you be? What will be the effect? How will they react? How personal should the information be? How much of my own personal life should I—dare I!—share? What if I feel too embarrassed to talk to my kids about sex? Will talking change our relationship? If so, how?

All these questions can and should be answered. Many of the answers can be found in the experiences of parents and teens who had the same fears, many of the same questions, but who did their best to try and begin talking to each other in spite of it.

Parents Do Talk about Sex

A survey was taken of 300 teens at a youth gathering. Of the 275 who actually filled out the survey, over 240 said that their parents did talk to them about sex. Yet nearly 200 of them said it was an awkward, sometimes embarrassing business. One survey question asked, "How often have your parents brought up issues of love, sex, or dating?"

The responses ranged from "Once in a great while" to "Very often—every time she gets paranoid!" It isn't hard to feel the frustration coming from both comments. Obviously, the one teen felt the conversations were all too few and far between.

The other comment betrays a good deal of fear on the part of a mother, which led her to bring up the issue. All of these feelings are much too real and very much a part of talking about sexual issues.

Dating Leads to Talking

One issue that emerged very clearly as a reason for talking about sexuality was dating. Some typical responses to that "How often?" question were

- "Not very much, only when they seem concerned that I'm dating too seriously." (16-year-old female)
- "After I'm late from a date." (16-year-old male)
- "Quite a lot, but mostly before or after a date." (15-year-old female)
- "Every time I go on a date." (16-year-old male)
- "After every date." (15-year-old female)
- "Not that much, except when I date." (16-year-old female)

One especially descriptive response to "How often have your parents brought up issues of love, sex, or dating?" came from a 17-year-old female: ' "Who is it?' and when we come back, 'What did you do?' in detail!"

Dating Deals with Sexual Reality!

It's not hard to understand why parents who normally would not bring up subjects connected with love, sex, or dating, do so when their son or daughter dates. Sexuality is then no longer theoretical or distant. When kids start to date, it becomes very real, very personal and very current.

The 17-year-old female quoted above also wrote in another part of the survey, "I choose not to talk to my parents because they fly off the handle!"

A 15-year-old female commented in the survey "I mostly discuss everything that I do with my parents, but some things I don't, because I like to keep some things to myself!"

This comment from a 16-year-old male was echoed by many, "I don't talk to my parents much because I'm afraid they'll laugh."

Dating becomes an important time for teens and parents to talk, but the talking has to be caring, sensitive, and respectful! Many teens are as sensitive as parents in talking about the issues. Most won't risk bringing up the subject themselves if they have to face anger, teasing, probing, or put-downs!

Attitudes Can Be a Barrier

"They think I'm too young to handle anything. I'm the baby and they want me to stay that way," are the words of a 15-year-old female.

"I'm afraid to talk to them because I'm a bit embarrassed, and they don't understand me. They think that almost every guy I like is no good!" This defensive comment came from another 15-year-old female.

"I can't talk to my parents because they just get all embarrassed and make me feel stupid!"

"They like to embarrass me a lot about those kinds of things. If I ask, they wonder what's wrong with me. They'd think I was weird or something." Both statements are from 16-year-old females.

"I don't feel I could talk seriously with them. I'm also afraid they'll not like the person I want to go out with," wrote a 17-year-old female.

It doesn't take long to see that the problem is not just with parents' attitudes. Many young people are frightened to reveal their real feelings and attitudes to their parents because they are uncertain of their parents' reaction as well as their own feelings. The need to find a way to start talking is forcefully and frighteningly evident. The need to get past judgments and assumptions is crucial.

This comment of a 16-year-old female sums up the need. "I can't talk to them, because it's embarrassing, and they have different ideas than I do. They want me to do better than they did!" That kind of unrealistic expectation from parents just cries out for help. The need for parents and young people to talk, listen, care, and support each other is critical!

For Some It Works Well

There were in the same brief survey a number of young people who spoke warmly of a parent-teen relationship that was very supportive. For these young people, talking about sexual issues seemed very possible and very natural. They expressed a rather confident feeling and seemed at ease with one or both parents. A 15-year-old male wrote, "I have no problem talking to Dad, but I'm not as close to my mom."

"It's easy to talk with my parents. They care about me"—this from another 15-year-old male.

A 16-year-old male wrote, "My parents taught me to look at a person's inward ways and thoughts, not their outward physical appearance. . . . My parents are very understanding and reasonable."

A 17-year-old female commented, "My mother and I talk a lot about all issues. It's not hard to talk to my parents. They understand me!"

Relationship Makes It Easier

What comes clearly through the written responses of these young people is that the relationship established between parents and teens makes the difference. Where they felt accepted as people, not judged or belittled, they expressed little fear of listening to what their parents said about most things, including sexuality. When they expressed confidence that their parents understood them, they seemed quite open to approaching their parents with most, if not all, issues.

What Does This Mean?

Luther's marvelous all-purpose catechism question serves very well here. What does all this mean? What does it mean that some parents and young people find it possible to talk about God's precious gift of sexuality with each other and some find it nearly impossible? What does it mean that some styles of relationships open the doors for healthy communication, and other styles seem to keep them shut? It means we live in a real world. It means that Satan is alive and working well to tear apart what God would build up. He makes difficult the very things God sees as essential.

Sexuality is not something neutral. It is a precious gift from God just as faith is His gift to us. Using the gift of sexuality well is part of the Christian's life as a steward of all God's gifts. To use sexuality well is to honor God and His Word. To abuse sexuality is to dishonor God and His Word. Is it any wonder that Satan works so hard to tarnish the gift, and confuse those who would follow the Giver? If he can discredit the gift and the way we use it, he can discredit the Giver! And all of this means . . .

There Is a Great Need

. . . to share the truth of our God about the gift of sexuality, what it is, what it means, and how God would have us use it.

- "Train a child in the way he should go" (Prov. 22:6).
- "Bring them up in the training and instruction of the Lord" (Eph. 6:4).
- "Teaching them to obey everything I have commanded you" (Matt. 28:20).
- "And how from infancy you have known the holy Scriptures which are able to make you wise for salvation" (2 Tim. 3:15).
- "All Scripture is God-breathed and is useful for teaching, rebuking, correcting and training in righteousness" (2 Tim. 3:16).

Scripture is filled with directives to God's people to teach and learn, train and instruct, so that each of us might know and live the will and ways of our gracious God. That teaching and learning is to include all of the truths God has revealed to us, including His truth regarding His gift of sexuality.

Male and Femaleness a Gift

How clear God makes it in Scripture that sexuality was His idea! Genesis 2 tells the story of a God who didn't want man to be alone, but wanted a "helpmate" for him. Not finding one among the animals, God fashioned a woman, made from Adam's rib. Acting as the first father of the bride, God presented Eve to Adam. What a picture, a gift from the Giver of all! Adam's recognition of that gift was clear and quick, "This is now bone of my bones and flesh of my flesh; she shall be called woman, for she was taken out of man. For this reason a man will leave his father and mother and be united to his wife, and they will become one flesh"(Gen. 2:23–24). St. Paul looks back to this giving at creation when he says, "Husbands, love your wives, just as Christ loved the church and gave himself up for her. . . . In this same way, husbands ought to love their wives as their own bodies. He who loves his wife loves himself. . . . However, each one of you also must love his wife as he loves himself, and the wife must respect her husband" (Eph. 5:25, 28, 33).

These words present a picture of man and woman, brought together in marriage by a loving God, committed to that God and to each other. What a clear picture they give of God's design for His gift of sexuality, that man and woman come together as one flesh, loving and cherishing each other as gifts that they are to each other.

Caring Is God's Kind of Love

There's only one word that describes that kind of love—caring. God's intent for us is that we experience and offer just that kind of cherishing, honoring, supporting, self-sacrificing love that rightly is called caring. That kind of love cares for more than self. It cares for the other. It is concerned about effects and outcomes. 1 Corinthians 13 gives wonderful detailed expression to that kind of love:

"It is not proud. . . .not self-seeking. . . .does not delight in evil but rejoices with the truth." That kind of love is not only God's invention, but God's intention for His people. To teach that love as the responsible expression of love of a man for a woman and woman for man is our responsibility and privilege as Christians. To hold out that high model of love between the sexes as God's plan for His people is our calling and duty.

Conquering Is the World's kind of Love

There is a great need to teach clear Christian values regarding sexuality because the world is teaching its own values. The world we live in isn't into caring; it's into conquering! If you have just a little bit of hesitation as to the need to talk to young people about a Christian perspective on sexuality, then just step into the corner drug store or an all-night grocery store or a magazine shop that has the always obvious magazine rack! Walk down the aisle and eye the magazines. It's all there, the bosoms and the biceps. They're in full color, men and women posed and poised, only partly clad, looking like so much meat on a hook. The message is there, "Everyone's doing it!" "Don't miss out on the action!" "Sex is there, it's available, and it's for the asking!"

If you still have doubts, pick up one of those magazines and read a story. It will use the word *love,* but it will have little resemblance to God's kind of love between man and woman. Sex is treated as a toy, not a treasure. Sex is for enticing, manipulating, taking, and using! There is nothing to suggest concern, cherishing, or commitment. There is nothing that sounds like caring. It's all conquering! It's all meeting my need, having my good time, getting my thrills!—not caring at all, only conquering!

Your teens and mine live in a world that takes that image very, very seriously. If the magazine rack doesn't convince you, just turn on the TV. Nine thousand sex scenes are available per year on television according to the National Federation for Decency. Sadly enough, a *Playboy* magazine source puts the estimate closer to 20,000 per year.

Add a quick review of magazine advertisements. Throw in a hearing of just a few selected rock lyrics and you can get the message loud and clear. Sex is a toy!

There is of course a new sober note sounded today. AIDS has made some people more cautious, if not more moral. "Safe sex" is now recommended. Some have even publicly advocated abstinence. But no public voice yet raises the issue of respect for one's own body, respect for the other person as a child of God, let alone love for God and His will, as reasons to place the full sexual exchange within the boundaries of committed love in marriage. The voice that proclaims sex to be the God-given gift and treasure that it is, is not heard in the public media or any public arena! Conquering is in, not caring!

Youth Get the Message

Little of this is lost on young people. In the absence of any consistent Christian message regarding sexual values they assume the obvious. They conclude that the values of the culture in sexual matters must be more or less supported by the Christian church, since the church says so little. They seem to write off any differences between their views and their parents' views as "old-fashioned," rather than moral. Research by Search Institute in Minneapolis, Minn., reveals little or no difference between young people who are church members and the general nonchurch population on sexual matters. As one privileged to talk to groups of young people in many places around the United States and Canada over the past 15 years, I continually hear the kinds of questions that our sex-as-a-toy culture produces.

"Why do guys only want sex?" "Why don't they care about your personality?" "Why don't they just want to be friends?" Those are the questions that teenage young women constantly ask. They are often angry, at times mildly confused, and frequently disgusted at the sexual pressure they receive from males. It's not hard to see that much of the time, many of those males are taking their cues for sexual values from the culture, not from a clear understanding of their faith!

Often the questions young males raise even in mixed audiences give painful evidence of the confusion our culture has created in them. "Why do girls dress so seductively and then back off on a date?" came from a 16-year-old male at a Lutheran youth gathering in a workshop on love, sex, and dating. Obviously, he interpreted what he perceived as being seductive dress (and perhaps most would consider it such) as signaling a person who was sexually aggressive, surely not one who would back off in response to his apparent sexual advances.

Another male, 17 years of age, at the same event asked in an unquestionably serious manner, "Why don't girls just relax and enjoy sex? I don't understand why they get so uptight!"

A 17-year-old female wrote in a survey, "I don't ever talk to my parents about sex. They don't think you should have sex before you're married!" In the same survey, the response came from a 16-year-old female, "I can't say anything to my parents about sex. They'd just get mad if they knew!"

It's hard to escape the reality that many of our young people in Christian homes base their sexual values on the culture around them. Some seem to have no clear support for Christian values. Others simply write off any view from home that seems to oppose the overwhelming message coming from the world around them.

How to Begin?

For the parent who has never brought up the subject of Christian values related to love, sex, or dating, it's important to give it more than a little thought before jumping in. It's important to involve both spouses if at all possible. Even in divorced or separated situations, it can be crucial to get the understanding and support of both parents.

Begin with Homework!

Strange as it sounds, reading key materials can be a great help in approaching your teens. The Sex Education series of Concordia Publishing House offers several volumes that are unusually helpful for the parents of teens. *How to Talk Confidently with Your Child about Sex* (previously titled *Sexuality, God's Precious Gift to Parents and Children*) is a good place to begin. It deals with some of the questions many parents have about talking to their children of all ages. It gives direction and support. A thorough review of the miracle of reproduction is presented at the adult level. How important for all of us as parents to appreciate again the incredible miracle of God we participate in when He allows us to bring children into the world!

This helpful volume begins offering age-by-age hints for talking to children and young people about sexuality by answering questions and offering suggestions. The junior high and high school years are covered as well. Hearing other Christian parents share their views and experiences when talking with their own children is most helpful as you begin your own first efforts.

Get the Teen's Perspective

To get a view "from their side of the fence," you will find it helpful to look into two other books from the Concordia series, *Sex and the New You* (previously titled *The New You*), for junior high young people, and *Love, Sex, and God* (previously titled *Lord of Life, Lord of Me*), written for high school age. These books speak to youth. They deal with the issues from the perspective of growing-into and learning-about oneself, and one's emerging sexuality. It's helpful (as difficult as it may seem) to try to see it from their standpoint. These and other similar books can help do just that. They will take you back and help you remember what it was like to have mostly questions but seemingly few answers.

Sex Relationships

Sex, Love, or Infatuation: How Can I Really Know? by Ray G. Short (Augsburg, 1978), is an excellent book to help you as a parent looking at the critical issues of male-female relationships. This little volume, available from most Christian bookstores, is written for young people. The author speaks candidly and accurately about the differences between sexual attraction, infatuation, and real love. It helps young people deal with that impossible-to-answer question, Am I in love? It serves a double purpose also by helping conscientious parents who want to think through those very issues with their son or daughter.

The book is now also available in Christian bookstores in a 50-minute videotape version. It features the author, Ray Short, sharing the content of his book in a studio presentation as well as before a live audience of young adults. It is an excellent discussion tool to help parents and young people deal with the real life issues of sexual responsibility. Parents, too, will find both the book and the tape informative. Young people appreciate the candor of the speaker, not to mention the courage of their parents in providing it.

Listening Can Help You Begin!

Spending considerable time listening to young people can be very profitable. It helps to know what they are saying, thinking, and feeling about sexual issues. Watching television with your teens can give you many opportunities to listen to their comments and reactions about sexuality. Listening can help you tune in to how they think about sex, how openly or comfortably they do, or don't, talk about it.

Listening first, with little comment, correction, or criticism may be very important, just to get a realistic sense of where they are. This kind of listening may give you that opening or clue as to how to begin.

One Place to Begin—Ask a Question!

After listening to the kinds of conversation your teens have about sexuality, a question might be the natural beginning point. For example, if your teenage daughter has been talking with a friend, complaining about the kind of jokes some of the guys at school are telling, your opening might sound something like this: "Joanne, I heard you talking with Sue earlier about the guys at school and their jokes about sex. I was wondering if all of the fellows are that way, or whether some are more responsible? Do you mind my asking?" That kind of question might open the door for some information-sharing that could be very helpful. The question as phrased respects your daughter's judgment. Most important, it asks permission to talk about the issue.

Another Place to Begin—Share a Concern!

Suppose your 15-year-old son is watching a television program on adolescent pregnancy. Even though he's watching the program with half an eye while paging through the sports section of the newspaper, you hear a comment from him every once in a while. Finally he blurts out, "Well, any gal dumb enough to get herself in that situation deserves what she gets!" Concerned as to just what your son does mean by that comment, you could say it something like this: "Jack, I'm not sure I know what you mean when you react like that. Would you mind telling me more about how you see this situation? I'd really like to know!"

Just that kind of simple question could open the door to your son's thinking. It might also give you the chance to share some of your values about sexuality. Your tone of voice and willingness to listen are needed to reassure him that you do want to hear his opinion, that you will not judge and condemn quickly, and that you are interested in hearing his views.

Something Looks Suspicious!

Always difficult for parents is the case where you sense trouble. Parents and teens have different values! Your teens see situations differently than you do at times. How do you handle situations that look compromising or dangerous for your teens?

Suppose your 16-year-old son has been invited to a friend's home for a party. Three days before the party you hear from another parent that no adult will be home the evening of that party. A day later you find out that only couples that have been dating seriously, including your son, have been invited as well. Even a parent who wants to put the best construction on everything has to face reality. This can be a situation that will put a great deal of sexual pressure on your son. To back away and just hope everything will be all right is to do nothing, is to shirk your responsibility, and frankly is not recommended by this writer, a parent of five teens. It's the time to approach the son kindly but realistically and share an honest concern.

Your opening might sound like this: "Jerry, can you help me out with some information about the party coming up. I've heard that Jack's parents will be out of town and only couples are invited. These may just be rumors, but I'd sure like to hear from you about it. I'm concerned about what you and Shelley might be walking into!"

Be Willing to Talk!

You just may have interrupted some carefully thought out plans by both your teenage son and his girl friend. On the other hand, you may have just offered your son and his girlfriend an opportunity to talk about a situation they were somewhat pressured into and didn't really think through. At any rate, raising questions is not a hit and run proposition. Raising the question means you will commit yourself to spend time and be willing to dialogue. Having raised the issue, it is now time to listen carefully to your son's responses. The opportunity to help him become a responsible steward is right there.

Merton Strommen in his classic book on youth ministry, *Bridging the Gap, Youth and Adults in the Church* (Minneapolis: Augsburg, 1973), offers three guidelines for talking to teens. Intended for adult youth leaders, his suggestions are most useful for parents, too, who must help young people deal with these important issues. Number one, writes Strommen, speak to your teens "as one trying to understand them." We parents find it so tempting to speak as one trying to correct, control, or confront them. The need is to understand their thoughts, their hopes, and their dreams.

Secondly, Strommen comments, speak to your teens "as one involved in life," not as one standing off to the side, watching life go by. Young people are bustling, active participants. They appreciate your involvement with them. They have a hard time respecting inactivity. Speaking out of your involvement lets them know that you are with them, struggling to be responsible yourself, not just demanding it of them.

Finally he writes, speak to your teens as "one with a hopeful view of the future." How important that God's people talk about the positive, hopeful approach to life that God gives. Even problems and conflicts can be dealt with in a hopeful manner, because we know His love, His forgiveness, and His promises. Seemingly insurmountable obstacles can be approached confidently because we know and trust His presence with us in all we do. That hope is crucial. To share that hope and speak out of that hope to our young people demonstrates that faith is amazingly practical for handling every problem in life.

And Then Comes the Conflict!

What if a conflict emerges? What if our questions and concerns voiced to our young people are met with "Yeah, we have slept together! So what! We love each other! Everybody's doing it!"

Dr. Earl Gaulke in his book, *You Can Have a Family Where Everybody Wins!*, (St. Louis: Concordia Publishing House, 1975), illustrates a wrenching conflict of values between a Christian father and daughter. Pam is living with her boyfriend, Johnny. The father has found out about it and has decided to confront his daughter with it. Here is the dialogue.

Parent: "Pam, what really concerns me about your sleeping with Johnny is what this is doing to your relationship with Christ."

Pam: "But, Dad, I love him—and I really don't think it's any of your business. It's not hurting you—and it won't. I always take the pill."

Parent: "You love Johnny—and you feel that's the important thing. I guess I can understand how you feel, but I sure can't accept it. I really feel awful about this. I feel that I've failed as a Christian parent."

Pam: "So don't try that 'poor Dad!' on me. It's my decision—mine and Johnny's."

Parent: "O.K. You feel that I'm trying to make a decision for you. Maybe I am—but I don't want to. To be honest with you, I'd like to see you make that decision for yourself. And I suppose I've got other feelings too, like, 'What would our friends think—of you and of us?' I really feel *ashamed*—for you and for us, your parents. But down underneath it all, my real and basic concern is about what's happening to your faith. I just don't see how you can be a Christian—and still persist in what you yourself know is wrong."

Pam: "I don't feel it's wrong. Just sleeping with any boy—yeah, that would be wrong. But Johnny and I really care for each other. Isn't that what makes sex good—and even beautiful? How about all the married people who don't care about each other—what's so good and holy about that? How about you and Mom—you don't have a perfect marriage! That's your business, and this is mine."

Parent: "Wow! You really do feel strongly about this. And so do I. Let me try to sort out where we're at. I'm relieved to hear how you feel about 'just sleeping with any boy.' That sure fits with the kind of person I know you are. And you love Johnny—that's the important thing for you. I can sure affirm that value too. So what it boils down to is that you feel it's O.K. to have premarital sex if you're in love. And I can't buy that value at all."

Pam: "Yeah."

Parent: "So how can we resolve this? Would you be willing to do some Bible searching with me—to see just what God's Word has to say about it?"

Pam: "I don't know. I guess that would be O.K.—as long as you don't preach at me."

Parent: "I don't want to preach. And you can stop me if I do. What we'd do is look up the verses that talk about sexual relations—and marriage—and let them speak to both of us. We could use your confirmation Bible, the one with the concordance. I'd sure feel good if you'd be willing to do that."

Pam: "O.K. Let's try" (pp. 79–80).

It's not easy to read that kind of dialogue. It tears at the innards of all Christian parents when they see that the values of their own flesh and blood offend the will of a gracious God. Even knowing and recalling our own sins and weaknesses doesn't soften the blow when our own kids fall victim to some of the world's pet sins. Yet with all the pain, this parent showed a very responsible way to deal with the situation.

Our responsibility as parents is surely to correct our young people when appropriate, but it is far more than that! Our job is to equip those young people to grow in distinguishing right behavior from wrong. Our task is more than just pointing out wrong. It is to help them develop greater confidence in their ability to sort out wrong from right, and that means getting them into the Word. It's the Word, blessed by the Spirit, that will teach, correct, and convict of wrong. It is also that same Word of God that can speak to a repentant heart and bring a message of forgiveness, renewal and restoration. Values are not formed by demands or commands from parents. They are formed as parents lead young people to the Word so that the shaping, changing power of the Word is brought to bear on the life, the faith, and the sexuality of that young person.

A Final Word

Don't be afraid to speak that Word! Don't hold back from

inviting your son or daughter to dig into the Word with you, to stand there together under the power of the Word. Speak and listen to understand, most surely. But speak as one filled with the hope of our God whose Word does touch and shape our lives. And speak as one involved, by God's grace, in a life lived as God's very own, out there in the very real world.

Speak, as one who knows the truth—about life, about faith, and about sexuality.

Share your life with your teen. Demonstrate in that life your clear commitment, that the gift of sexuality is not a toy at all, but a precious gift from a gracious loving Heavenly Father.

God will bless that effort. And that effort on your part will be a blessing to your teens, rest assured!

Points to Remember

1. It's the relationship between parent and teen that makes the difference.
2. God's kind of love is caring rather than conquering.
3. Parents need to teach clear Christian values about sexuality.
4. Many young people base their understanding of sex on the teachings of culture rather than on parents or Scriptural teachings.
5. In order to teach a proper understanding of sex and sexuality, parents need to understand sex themselves.
6. Understand the teen's perspective about sex and sexuality.
7. Play a listener's role and learn how to ask questions to open the door to conversation.
8. Do not hesitate to express concerns.
9. Be willing to talk!
10. Speak
    as one trying to understand;
    as one involved in life; and
    as one with a hopeful view of the future.
11. Speak God's Word!

The Three R's of Teen Sexuality

Jean Garton

ugust 1987

Dear Donn:

    This has been quite a year for you, hasn't it? A high school graduation, enrollment as a college freshman, and this month a very special teen birthday. Happy number 18!

    It is turning out to be an unusual year for me, too, as I experience an "empty nest" and recognize that, although still a teen, my "baby" is well on his way to manhood. As a result, the last four years we shared ("struggled through" might be more accurate) have been on my mind. How could I have prepared you better? What more could I have done or said to nurture the potential and the beauty that God has placed in you?

    The time to "parent" you has gone by too quickly, and now

you're off to college. But you are very much in my thoughts today as I sit here at the typewriter because, as the saying goes, a funny thing happened to me on the way to your high school graduation.

Amid all the cards of congratulations that arrived for you was a letter to me with an invitation to write a chapter for a book about parents, teens, and social issues. My particular chapter was to address ''Helping Parents Talk to Teens about Teenage Pregnancy.''

By now you have to be laughing! Remembering all of my unsuccessful attempts to talk to you on that subject (which dead-ended with your ''Aw, Mom'' and hasty retreat from the room), you probably think I'm the least likely candidate to author such a chapter. Wrong! We've talked more often than you realize, although during these teen years my talking has had to be more indirect.

Remember the time you asked if I had any material on how conception occurs? There you stood—a tall, handsome, healthy 17-year-old—asking about pregnancy. My heart did a flip-flop as I attempted a casual, if somewhat high-pitched, ''Why do you want to know?''

As it turned out, you had a health class assignment on the topic, and I suspect my relief showed as I over-enthusiastically gathered up brochures, books, and pictures. During those days of providing information for your report I had an opportunity—in an objective, unemotional way—to talk about the wonder and responsibility of creating new life. (You received an A from the teacher, I recall, who thought your video-taped report was ''creatively informative.'' I gave myself an A, too, for being ''creatively informative'' by finding a way to talk with you about teenage pregnancy that was natural and pertinent to the situation at hand.

Parents aren't as dumb as some experts and teens think! Frustrated, yes, because we really love you and genuinely want to help you. We know, though, that parents are the last ones to whom most teenagers listen, and we can quickly sense your built-in resistance to our advice. We know, too, that various forms of rebellion and adjustment difficulties are common during this period of a young person's life. After all, we were teenagers ourselves once upon a time and can remember the struggle of those years to develop our own identities.

I know you always groan when I start to talk about what it

was like in "my day." (I'll remind you of that when you become a parent and say the same thing!) It's not just that I've come to have an adult perspective about things but that it really was different in those days. We've come a long way since teens labored over whether or not to kiss a date good-night, when "easy" was a description that struck terror in the hearts of teenaged girls. Teens lived together back then but usually *after* marriage . . . and got pregnant, too, but *after* marriage.

Actually, I was one of those "educationally deprived" kids who went through 12 years of public school without any classes in sex education. (Is it just a coincidence, do you think, that there was no such thing then as a teen pregnancy crisis or national epidemic?) It seems to me that the lack of restraint in your generation has spawned as many (and more serious) problems as did the so-called lack of honesty and openness in my day.

It is clear that in recent years both the rules and the roles have changed and, frankly, given a choice between walking through a mine field and helping parents talk to young people about teenage pregnancy, I'd probably choose the mine field. Shakespeare said it well: "I can easier teach twenty what were good to be done, than be one of twenty to follow mine own teaching."

Parents sometimes find it harder to talk about this subject than their kids. One reason is that many adults have lost confidence in their ability to parent. They have come to feel less qualified to guide and direct their children than the so-called experts who have become, in a real sense, "professional parents" of their children.

However, I believe it more dangerous than a mine field for teenagers, the family, and society to continue the current practice of diminishing the influence of parents on their children. As a mother who has somehow muddled through the teen years of four children (and lived to tell about it), I recognize the fact that minor children do have rights. But, Donn, parents have rights, too!

One right which has eroded is the right to know when our children are embarking on a course that is hazardous to their health and well-being. (Remember how testy you became when a neighbor kid tried to get John to climb a tree? Never mind that John was just a dog! You knew it wasn't safe, and when you saw him tottering on the branch you quickly and angrily intervened. After all, he was *your* pet and *your* responsibility.)

The rights parents have are God-given and include the right to be the primary shapers of their children's values and morals, especially in matters of sexual activity. You thought I was overreacting, didn't you, when I learned that one of the programs during your orientation at college was conducted by a sex therapist. "Mom's bent out of shape," was the way you put it. You bet I was! Your Dad and I have mortgaged our future for the next four years to get you an education but *not* in "Groinocology" as that lecture was billed.

Teens, on the other hand, have a right to know what parents believe is right. So, Donn, here goes! Your Mom's three R's for talking about teenage pregnancy: Realities, Responsibilities, and Restraint.

Reality number 1 is that sex is big business! In an average year of television-watching you see 10,000 references to sex—and none of them deals with the idea of consequences. The seductive message of advertising, for instance, encourages you to value sexual desirability above everything else. From jeans to cars, from deodorants to toothpaste, products are promoted with the implied message that they will provide you with sex and that sex means fun.

I remember addressing a class of seventh and eight graders in an expensive, private school where the students presented me with what they called their "position paper on sexual rights." Among other things it said the following:

If a couple is engaged in "procreational" sex, that is, they intend to have a family, then an abortion would be wrong. But if they are engaged in "recreational" sex—as we are (those seventh and eight graders!)—then an abortion would be perfectly all right because what we intend is fun and not a family.

They, as many adults, thought they could somehow separate what *they* do from what their bodies do, ignoring the Biblical truth that what we do in our bodies is done by us (1 Cor. 6:18–20).

Think of all the money to be made off teenagers in terms of salaries for those who promote such raw pleasure principles. Think of the funds expended for contraceptives and abortions. Think of the entrepreneurs in the family planning business, many of which are tax-supported agencies, funded according to the number of "clients" they "treat."

It is in the interests of many people to promote the beliefs that (1) sex is foremost in the minds of teenagers and (2) that "everybody's doing it." Neither is true!

The idea that sexual involvement dominates the thoughts of teenagers is not born out by research. Various studies in the area of thought-sampling were publicized at the 1987 annual meeting of the American Psychological Association. The data demonstrated that sex occupied only about 1 percent of the thoughts of both high school and college students while more than 27 percent of their thoughts concerned other people and 20 percent was devoted to the task at hand. That's hardly evidence that you teens are obsessed with sex and are not capable of controlling yourselves.

So who's creating the tremendous pressure for you to be part of the everybody's-doing-it crowd? The reality is that not only has sex become a form of intimidation and propaganda, but teens have become a lucrative and exploitable market. That really hits my hot button!

Some years ago I attended a government-sponsored conference on teenage pregnancy. Representatives of the leading family planning businesses in the U.S. said throughout the meeting that "kids know about contraceptives and have access to them, so why aren't our programs working?" One of their colleagues responded by saying, "What do you mean our programs aren't working! *We're* employed, aren't we?"

The reality is that teen sexuality and teen pregnancy are marketable commodities. No wonder so many people have an interest in encouraging an active sex life for teens. But parents aren't among them, Donn. I know that when business is good for them, it's bad for you because reality number 2 is that teen sex is a health hazard.

Sexual intercourse carries with it a load of emotional and psychological baggage that ought to be part of a committed and permanent relationship. Further, there are also physical problems connected with teenage sexual activity. It has come as a surprise, for instance, that cervical cancer and cervical abnormalities arising later in life have as one clearly established cause frequent intercourse with a variety of partners, especially if begun in adolescence.

Then there are the varied kinds of venereal diseases which, contrary to popular perception, are not always diagnosed and treated in time to prevent permanent injury and that are almost certainly passed on if a boy or girl has several partners.

I remember visiting the famous Mayo Clinic in Minnesota which, for some people, is a place of last resort. They go there seeking, in a sense, a miracle, and some find one. A high school senior I met was not among them.

I had left the tour group to locate a restroom and entered to find the young woman sobbing as she sat crumpled on the floor.

She had traveled from a distant state, confident that she would find at Mayo the cure her physicians at home could not provide. She had just been told, however, that there was no cure for herpes—not for her, not for anyone, not anywhere in the world.

Is premarital sex worth the risk of permanent venereal disease or the risk of hurt that will be caused to one's self and one's family? Given the current AIDS epidemic, is sex something you're willing to die for? Is a few moments of "fun" worth the possibilty of an unwanted pregnancy? Teenage girls who get abortions number about 400,000 each year. Is sex something you're willing to kill for? The truth is that when you reject God's best for you—sex and pregnancy within marriage—every other choice is second best.

Reality number 3 is that while teen pregnancy does exist in unprecedented numbers, and for many complex reasons, it is not a disaster for all young people who are included in the so-called "teen pregnancy epidemic." The assertion that each year over a million teenage girls become pregnant can be misleading, since over a third of those teens were married at the time the pregnancy occurred and a substantial percentage of the rest married upon finding out they were pregnant.

Have you ever wondered—if one million teenage girls "become pregnant" each year—what their partners, teenage boys, "become"? "Absent mostly," those girls tell us. Many realize too late that although a relationship was "meaningful" to them, it turned out to be sheer self-satisfaction on the part of the other. Boys, on the other hand, said that "a meaningful relationship" often becomes so meaningful for some girls that they want to cement that relationship with a child.

The reality is that each sex is misusing the other. There are other important differences between males and females than simply the "plumbing and equipment." Your sex drive, Donn, as a young man, peaked at 17. Your sisters', however, as females, did not peak until about age 27. Teen boys have a strong sex drive, and teen girls have a strong love drive. So a boy uses love to get sex, and a girl uses sex to get love; and, in the process, they misuse each other. Sometimes a new life is created as a result.

That 400,000 teenagers a year choose to deal with those pregnancies by aborting their unborn children should be seen as another horrifying symptom (rather than a cure) that the lowest and most debased values have been transmitted to your generation. Abortion buries a problem—in more ways than one.

What abortion does is curb births, not pregnancies. Yet many sex education programs promote contraceptive devices and pills as a means of practicing "responsible sex" or "safe sex." Using contraceptives doesn't make teen sex responsible. Avoiding pregnancy doesn't make sex responsible. Terminating a pregnancy doesn't make sex responsible. (None of those make for safe sex either! As Dr. James Dobson said: There is no "safe" sex any more than there is "safe" sin.)

Donn, premarital sex isn't wrong because a young person might get pregnant. It's wrong because your body is a temple that belongs to God. *And* so does that other body—the new, tiny, living, unborn body that exists in every teenage pregnancy!

We're not talking "recreation" here! We're talking Responsibility with a capital R. Remember the teacher in your school who required every student in her class to carry around an egg (not hard-boiled either) for a certain period of time? She wanted to give teens a little hint of what it's like to be totally responsible for the well-being—for the very existence—of another.

Responsibility is in short supply among us adults as well as among young people. No wonder you are having such a hard time learning and living it. Ted Koppel, the news commentator, said recently that "as far as children are concerned, parents stand in the place of God. What a strange conclusion—us, in the place of God. We, who set such flawed examples for you."

He's right! We make mistakes, for instance, in what we say

and are not as responsible with words as we should be. Sometimes, unwittingly and unconsciously, we condition young people to complicate the problem of an unwanted pregnancy by having them seek an abortion. You and I both know of kids who have said, "I couldn't tell my dad I'm pregnant—he'd throw me out." Or, "I couldn't tell my mom I'm pregnant—it would kill her."

Since many teens have been raised with a value system that includes discipline and obedience, they have grown up with an unwritten Eleventh Commandment: Never Hurt Mom or Dad. Thus, some young people feel morally justified—or even compelled—to have a secret abortion to "protect" Mom or Dad from pain and hurt.

It's easy to spot the threats young people have heard (or thought they heard) from their parents. Usually those words really aren't meant but are a verbalization of parents' sense of helplessness in the face of a potential threat to their teen's health and future. The perception many teens have as a result of such words, though, is of a father who severely lacks compassion and understanding and of a mother so weak and fragile she would collapse at the news. Well, maybe she would but not for long. Mothers are resilient creatures. Count on tears and maybe even anger, but give us a chance to show also our faith at work and our confidence in Christ's promise to always be with us. Because of His faithfulness to us, we can be faithful parents to you.

I think, therefore, that parents and teens have a responsibility to establish a common mechanism in order to explore each others' real (not perceived) feelings and understandings. *If* we would listen to you teenagers (and *if* you would talk to us!) we would discover that you do have values. You, in turn, would discover that we have both the courage and compassion to help you work through these problems.

We parents also have the responsibility to act upon the fact that young people want to know what they should believe in and what they ought to become. Because many Christian homes and Christian churches shut out the subject of teenage sex, many teens are experiencing heartbreak and tragedy. Our homes and congregations can be communities of grace where forgiveness is proclaimed and practiced because teen pregnancy is everybody's responsibility.

We all need to know some facts about it, though—teens, especially. Not just for yourself but because the first person a teen contacts is another teen. God can use you to help a friend avoid or cope with a pregnancy. Did you know, for instance, that some teenagers *want* to become pregnant? Sadly, their pregnancies result not from love but from an absence of love, not from caring but from an environment in which no one cared enough.

Many pregnant teens, in response to the question of how they came to be in that condition, convey a feeling that someone else did it to them: "My date got me drunk and I must have passed out," or, "My boyfriend would have been mad if I didn't do it." Generally, they demonstrated an inability to think out the consequences of their actions.

Statistics from states where parental involvement has been required for distribution of contraceptives and sex education indicate that pregnancy rates go down, not up.

Physical risks for pregnancy and delivery for females in the 15 to 17 age group are no greater than for women in their 20s provided the teenager receives medical attention during and after the pregnancy.

When an abortion is used as a "solution" to teenage pregnancy, the emotional effects can be devastating. While the immediate response tends to be one of relief, the long range effects have been documented as appearing between five to ten years after the procedure.

There is a quiet agony of the soul for many teens who have an abortion, particularly if it is without parental knowledge. In the majority of cases, they lose their boyfriends, lose their babies, and lose an open and trusting relationship with their families at a crucial time in their development.

Research documents that pregnancy and abortion can result in trauma for teenage males as well. (Donn, do you recall that letter I received from a young man in prison where he was serving a life sentence for murder? He wrote, "I have more guilt feelings about an abortion I paid for years ago than for the crime I am in here for now.")

Recent studies show that teenage pregnancy has less to do with contraceptive mechanics and sex education than with values, that the fundamental question facing young people is not "How do I avoid pregnancy?" but "Who and what am I?"

There's a lot more that could be added to the list, but experience demonstrates that facts don't really convince people to change behavior. Think of all the classes teens have had on drug and alcohol abuse and on the hazards of smoking. Millions hear those lectures and yet millions continue to ignore the facts. Educators themselves find it ludicrous to maintain that increasing information can alter behavior. Yet, in the area of sex education that is the dominating philosophy: more and more facts and earlier and earlier.

After years of talking with teens about preventing or experiencing an unwanted pregnancy, I have concluded that they would rather be given standards than contraceptives. In fact, at a government hearing on teenage pregnancy, one of the young women testifying said, "Why do they make it so easy for us?"

I remember, too, an incident at a center for pregnant teenagers where the teacher asked what they most would like to discuss. Child birth? Caring for a baby? Family planning methods? The young women showed little interest in any of those subjects. However, all hands shot up when the teacher asked, "Would you like to discuss how to say 'no' to your boyfriend without losing his love?"

Donn, as a teenaged young man, I hope you have a sensitivity to the great pressures placed on a teenaged girl. It is easy for a young man to take advantage of her feelings, easy to exploit her own feelings of being unloved at home or of not feeling good about herself. Yet, male teens, too, lose more than virginity when they engage in premarital sex.

I know a young man who said that one of the major things he lost was his self-respect, and that made him doubt his own self-control with other people. Also, he hadn't believed what he had heard about how casual sexual activity causes a desensitizing of a human being. Not, that is, until it happened to him. He said he deliberately became numb to how he had changed.

Another thing he lost, he said, was his spirituality which he described as "a separateness and emptiness" in his life. As with many teenagers raised in a Christian home, "religious things" had become unimportant to him. He hadn't realized how much comfort there was in having God in his life until he went from ignoring Him to deliberate disobedience of His Word.

From any perspective a person can think of, it appears that the effects of teenage pregnancy and the solutions to teenage pregnancy are far more difficult to handle than coping with the challenges of chastity.

Many don't even know what that word means anymore, much less see it as an achievable or desirable goal. In practice it means restraint—saying no—not now, not yet. But the purpose of chastity is not to prevent something but to enjoy something.

Remember that cartoon I tacked on the refrigerator? (One of my silent, if not subtle, hints!) It showed a teenage boy saying to his grandfather: "Gee, Granddad, your generation didn't have all these social diseases. What did you wear to have safe sex?" Without missing a beat, the older man said: "A wedding ring."

We are all—single and married, young and old—called to chaste living, and it doesn't help my blood pressure to read those T-shirts that advertise: *Some Do—Some Don't . . . Some Will—Some Won't . . . I Might.* Or to see the bumper stickers that say: *Thanks All You Virgins—For Nothing!* I want to tell Mr. Macho to find himself a cold shower because when he gets "nothing," she gets everything: Freedom from venereal disease . . . from complications associated with contraceptives . . . from unwanted pregnancy . . . from the risks of abortion . . . from guilt . . . and much, much more.

A moral amnesia has set into our society that hinders the building of healthy lives, families, and societies. We are quick to provide teens with the means for avoiding pregnancy; and if those fail, we provide abortion to avoid birth. Yet many teens are expressing feelings of guilt—guilt that comes from sin—and that's a big factor in teenage sex and teenage pregnancy.

It doesn't make sense to spend so little time on morality education and so much time on sex education. Simply put, we've domesticated the devil. Paraphrasing the words of a popular song from "My Fair Lady": We've grown accustomed to his face . . . accustomed to his smile . . . accustomed to his voice.

But Jesus is so powerful, more powerful, ultimately powerful when He is recognized in a person's life—particularly in one's sex life. Intercourse involves profound and mighty forces of love and life that are wonderful and blessed gifts from God. It is the most intimate physical expression of an individual's total giving of him or herself in the embrace of love. That kind of love isn't given for a half hour and then taken back. It is an exclusive and permanent kind of love that is intended for marriage. It is a kind of love so mighty that the Scriptures compare it to the love between Christ and His church (Eph. 5: 21–33).

That's the high calling and challenge confronting you teens today, Donn. All else is counterfeit and can rob you of the joy and beauty God intends for your life.

So, what do you think? Is that worth knowing about? You bet it is! Sure, you're biologically and physiologically old enough to play the "game" of sex, but you ought to know the ground rules:

- To have the right to choose demands the duty to choose well and to choose the truth.
- The truth is that the only 100 percent effective contraceptive is not an oral one (the pill) but a verbal one (It's OK to say NO!).
- You *can* decide where your life is going. You can be in control as to when and with whom you will have children.
- At the risk of stating the obvious, pregnancy does not descend on a person like the flu. It happens when a male and female engage in sexual intercourse.
- However, experimentation need not, and frequently does not, lead to regular sexual activity.
- A turnaround is possible and often achieved. Some call it "secondary virginity," a psychological concept.
- To look for control outside of self-control is to settle for what looks good rather than what is good.
- And what's really good is found in the Good News—that because of Christ's death and resurrection there is forgiveness even for premarital sex, for unmarried pregnancy, and for abortions.

Christ's blood was shed for you, Donn, for your Mom and for all the teens and parents who want to start over today regardless of what happened yesterday. That's the best help parents can have in talking to teens about anything!

With the confidence that Jesus is only a breath away, Donn,

my "pen runneth dry." It's time to close for now but not before I tell you that I love you. I'm not crazy about your messy room, your smelly sneakers, or your piles of laundry. But you? You I'm crazy about!

Your Mom

Some Thoughts for Parents

- If you abdicate your authority, who will be in the business of telling teens what is good for teens?
- Which better enriches the self-image of young people: giving them the pill and condom or giving them your time and wisdom?
- Does your own life-style help teens develop a "future time perspective" so they might see that decisions made today (about sex/no sex, about contraceptives/no contraceptives, about abortion/no abortion) are relevant to the rest of their lives?
- What is the effect on teens of holding up the ideal of sex and pregnancy within marriage and then by promoting conceptives implying it is not achievable?
- If your teenager entered the room now and announced that she was pregnant (or that he had made a girl pregnant), what would be the first words you would say?
- Would role-playing that situation help you to be prepared in the event it did occur? Given time to think about it when it is only hypothetical, would you be able to respond to the news in the way Jesus has responded to you and your sins: I love you and I forgive you.

Some Help for the Hurting

- *Rest.* "Be still, and know that I am God" (Ps. 46:10).
- *Repent.* "If we walk in the light, as he is in the light, we have fellowship with one another, and the blood of Jesus, his Son, purifies us from all sin" (1 John 1:7).
- *Request.* "Jesus stopped and called to them. 'What do you want me to do for you?' " (Matt. 20:32).
- *Respond.* "I can do everything through him [Christ] who gives me strength" (Phil. 4:13).
- *Rejoice.* "Always giving thanks to God the Father for everything" (Eph. 5:20).

- *Rejoice again!* "We know that in all things God works for the good of those who love him" (Rom. 8:28).

Points to Remember

1. Parents have God-given rights to be the primary shapers of their children's values and morals.
2. Sex is big business in our society but often does not deal with the consequences of sex.
3. Parents and teens share a responsibility to establish a common mechanism to explore each others feelings and understandings.
4. Teenage pregnancy has less to do with contraception and sex education than it does with values.
5. The purpose of chastity is not to prevent something but to enjoy something.
6. More time needs to be spent on morality education than on sex education.

Sexual Identity: Who Sets the Agenda?

Ron Brusius

Craig is 17 years old, an honor student, active in his church, liked by everybody, and until recently, the focus of his parents' hopes for the future. Craig has always been exceptional. Mom says, "I remember when he was a little baby. He was always so good. We never worried about him. He smiled early, noticed things around him early, began reading early. He's always loved books, art, and is really into computers. From the moment that he was born, I knew that he was special!"

Craig's mom and dad saw many of their dreams for the future crushed upon learning that Craig believes he is gay. When they first found out, their initial reaction was that it can't be. Then they started to think of Craig as dead. Their Craig died when replaced by a Craig who revealed a side they could not understand, accept, or even admit.

Very quickly they started looking for a counselor who could change Craig into a "normal" person again. Craig was willing to see counselors, do just about anything that his parents wanted him to do in order to restore peace in his family. Mom and Dad were afraid to talk to their pastor for fear that their friends and others in the congregation would find out. Their lives are now different and their relationship with each other is strained. Ultimately, Dad will want to write Craig off and get on with life. Mom will try to understand what is happening, try to reconcile Craig and Dad, and try to find some way to change Craig and make the nightmare go away.

Craig won't say much about his homosexuality, but he will look for openings to convert Mom and Dad to his point of view, even going so far as leaving prohomosexual literature around at home, hoping that Mom and Dad will see "how wrong they are." He does love them and wants to change them, so that they can be more accepting.

Craig is aware of the threat of AIDS but is not personally concerned about contacting it. He says that he has a "sense" which helps him pick sexual partners who are not carriers. Besides, he'll tell you, that he's attracted to homosexuals because they are more loving and caring than the people in his family and his church.

Craig's story is a story repeated in more homes than most would care to admit. In doing congregational presentations on sex and sexuality, I often say that at least four families in any given congregation are touched by homosexuality, no matter what size the congregation is. The figure four is a number that I chose arbitrarily. There are no reliable numbers on the incidence of homosexual behavior in our society. Most figures used are still based on the Kinsey estimates of about 10 percent of the male population and 2 to 4 percent of the female population being gay. However, I cannot recall a time after almost casually mentioning that four families are touched by homosexuality when I did not talk to at least one individual about a relative who is gay.

Homosexuality has been an issue in societies down through the ages. The treatment of homosexuals in cultures has varied from persecuting them and putting them to death to tolerating them. In the past, cultures labeled homosexuality as deviant behavior. What is happening in North American culture is that homosexual behavior is now promoted as alternate behavior on essentially the same level as heterosexual behavior.

The practical implications of this are staggering. Today it is almost impossible to define what a family is. The White House Conference on Families during President Carter's administration was almost scuttled because of the gay proponents who insisted that gay families are as natural a family form as the two-parent heterosexual family.

Gay groups argue for gay counselors to be called in to counsel with any high school student who believes he or she may be gay. They believe that it is a civil rights issue and that sexual preference and sexual practices should be afforded the same protection that race, religion, and gender are given.

Many parents object to so-called AIDS education on grounds that it presents homosexuality as acceptable behavior. They are right in so far as programs and materials are presented as value-free, but which take for granted that teens cannot be taught that abstinence is an acceptable alternative to being sexually-active, or which see homosexuality and heterosexuality as simply two equally viable options.

AIDS education is going on through the media, through formal and informal programs; and our young people are being educated about homosexuality whether we are involved in it or not. Craig's "sense" about sexual partners is typical of youths' optimism about their own instincts and abilities to not get caught. It also is a strong argument against scare tactics being the best motivator for producing changes in behavior.

Strong cases are made for both homosexual activity and for heterosexual activity outside of marriage in the most popular media—television and movies. Even shows which appear to support heterosexual activity within marriage as the preferred route often leave homosexuality as an acceptable option. The change in recent times since the AIDS scare is that to be responsible means to practice "safe sex," in other words certain precautions are to be taken while still engaging in the behavior.

The condom which was once discarded as unreliable and unsafe has risen to national prominence as a way to avoid AIDS while continuing essentially the same kinds of behavior. Since the acceptance of condoms—even by people who admit their limited effectiveness—standards on television have fallen even lower as comedians have included references to them in their jokes and as situation comedies began to promote safe sex rather than abstinence.

The changes in societal thinking and moral standards appear to be so drastic and so dramatic that many parents fear for their teens' future and despair over what lies ahead for them. The sinfulness of our age may be more open in many ways than other ages, but we are probably not terribly different from parents of earlier times. Each age has its moral contradictions. Today, for example, few groups will speak against chastity as the best way to prevent the spread of sexually transmitted diseases. However, few groups will hold it up as the only acceptable option, using arguments which say that we cannot expect young people to be chaste, therefore we must provide information through euphemistically named avenues such as school-based health clinics. While they speak of a certain standard on an ideal level, they also say that the ideal is not possible to achieve.

St. Paul is labeled by many as being anti-woman and anti-sex. This is far from the truth. St. Paul recognized the corruptness of the cultures in which he lived and ministered. Those cultures were no more godless than cultures today. In many ways, today's culture has separated God and culture more effectively than the Graeco-Roman world did. Those cultures had a wealth of gods who supported their immoral lives and sexual practices. What Paul condemned was an immorality which was integrated into society and even seen as acceptable behavior. How similar to what we encounter today!

What Does the Bible Say about Homosexuality?

The first reference to homosexual behavior is found in the familiar story of Sodom, Gen. 19:1–11. Two angels came to Lot to warn him about the impending destruction of Sodom and were urged to stay overnight at Lot's home. "Before they had gone to bed, all the men from every part of the city of Sodom—both young and old—surrounded the house. They called to Lot, 'Where are the men who came to you tonight? Bring them out to us so that we can have sex with them.' " Lot offered his two virgin daughters to the mob rather than letting them violate his guests. The mob refused, threatened Lot himself, and the result was that all of the men were struck blind. There can be no doubt that the men intended to rape the two visitors. The same language is used in other places to indicate sexual intercourse. Proponents of homosexuality argue that this section should not be used to prove that God condemns the homosexual inclinations of the Sodomites; instead it indicates that they were inhospitable to guests in their city and the real reason for the destruction of the city is its unbelief. There can be no doubt, however, that the incident points out the immorality of the residents of the city even if it is not a clear condemnation of homosexuality itself. The name of the city Sodom has been used through the centuries to indicate certain sexual acts.

Lev. 18:22–23 reads: "Do not lie with a man as one lies with a woman; that is detestable. Do not have sexual relations with an animal and defile yourself with it. A woman must not present herself to an animal to have sexual relations with it; that is a perversion." Clearly, these verses condemn homosexuality and bestiality as perversions and sins. Proponents of homosexuality do not deny these words. Instead, they ask that they be considered in the context of the other Levitical prohibitions and point out that many of those prohibitions such as those against eating pork, shellfish, and other meats were set aside. The implication, of course, is that homosexuality is not against God's natural laws.

Probably best-known are the words of Paul in Rom. 1:18–32 where we are told that even though people have knowledge of God written in their hearts, they choose to ignore that knowledge and worship the creature rather than the Creator. "Therefore God gave them over in the sinful desires of their hearts to sexual impurity for the degrading of their bodies with one another. They exchanged the truth of God for a lie, and worshiped and served created things rather than the Creator, who is for ever praised. Amen. Because of this, God gave them over to shameful lusts. Even their women exchanged natural relations for unnatural ones. In the same way the men also abandoned natural relations with women and were inflamed with lust for one another. Men committed indecent acts with other men, and received in themselves the due penalty for their perversion." Paul goes on to say that God "gave them over to a depraved mind," so that they were filled with all sorts of wickedness and continued in their ways even though they knew that such people deserve to die. There can be little doubt that one of the behaviors which God condemns here is homosexuality. Many proponents of homosexuality admit that this New Testament reference is a clear condemnation of homosexuality but explain it away by saying that this applies to people who were created as heterosexuals. It does not apply to those whom God has created as homosexual. Of course, this is a weak argument, since nowhere in Scripture do we see any evidence that God created male and female any way other than heterosexual in nature.

This section is also used as proof that homosexuals are damned. It certainly does state that this behavior of turning in on self can lead a person to worship himself or herself and rejects God. Often the homosexual who comes to a pastor or religious counselor knows that homosexuality is a sin and wants to escape the bondage which can result from being caught in this trap.

The other section which is often used as a proof that homosexuals are damned is 1 Cor. 6:9–11: "Do you not know that the wicked will not inherit the kingdom of God? Do not be deceived: Neither the sexually immoral nor idolators nor adulterers nor homosexual offenders nor thieves nor the greedy nor drunkards nor slanderers nor swindlers will inherit the kingdom of God. And that is what some of you were. But you were washed, you were sanctified, you were justified in the name of the Lord Jesus Christ and by the Spirit of our God." Homosexuality here is included as one of many sinful behaviors which exclude an individual from the kingdom of God. The emphasis of these passages is on new life in Jesus Christ and gives all of us hope that we are saved by grace and can put aside the bondage caused by our personal sinfulness. It is a clear call to forsake the old sinful ways with an emphasis on God's action for us!

It does little good to attempt to argue with someone on the basis of Scripture if he is convinced that homosexuality is acceptable behavior, unless that person is willing to agree that Scripture is the Word of God and does have relevance for life today just as surely as when it was first recorded. Scripture condemns homosexuality, just as it condemns all forms of sinful behavior. David was outraged when Nathan told him the story of the rich man stealing the poor man's one lamb and by the same token was overcome with guilt and remorse when Nathan told him that he had done just that by taking Bathsheba (2 Samuel 12). What we see today is a God-wouldn't-want-me-to-be-unhappy kind of mentality which can excuse the grossest of sinful behaviors under the guise of freedom. When the message condemns unacceptable behavior, modern day thinking says that it is time to change prophets, transfer churches, or drop out from the church. It is more popular to discredit the Word than change behavior!

Many theories attempt to explain or justify homosexuality. I remember being in a graduate school class where a paper was presented listing 31 different possible causes. In spite of what you may read or be told, no definite cause for homosexuality has been established. According to Frank Worthen, Director of Love in Action, a program in San Rafael for males who want to get out of the gay life-style, the scientific community still does not even have a consensus on the definition of homosexuality. Worthen rejects the popular theory today that some people are born gay.

Instead Worthen talks about a "preconditioning package" which, for some, combined with other factors will contribute to getting into a homosexual life-style. The factors Worthen identifies as keys in preconditioning are loneliness, no sense of belonging, and feelings of insecurity.

Parents often want to blame themselves for a teen who identifies as gay. However, if they can say that their relationship as husband and wife was good and that their child was loved, affirmed, and had a sense of belonging, there is probably little that they can do to ferret out the causes for the behavior.

I personally prefer to work with a theory which identifies homosexuality as a learned behavior. One of the most important ingredients is how the person sees himself or herself. This is so powerful that even people who have never had a sexual experience will be convinced that they are gay. A male in his mid-20s went from counselor to counselor looking for one who would tell him that he was gay, even though he had never spoken to a gay and was repulsed by gay sexual practices. He had dated a number of females—each one once. He would never ask for another date because he was sure that each one suspected that he was gay. A female college student in her late teens also thought she was gay because she masturbated regularly, had problems talking to males, and easily lost her temper, so she had few friends of either sex. Both of them had low social skills and both suffered from low self-esteem. In other words, they lacked the skills necessary to get along with other people and thought that there was something different about them which made it impossible for them to get along with other people. Looking for labels for why they couldn't get along with others, they accepted the homosexual label.

Male homosexuals may be people who possess low social skills and get involved in a gay community because they crave the support that they are given rather than the sexual activity it offers. The image of the homosexual is often of one who "cruises," looking for casual sexual contacts and even multiple contacts within a short period of time. This type of behavior is much less frequent since the onset of the AIDS epidemic. Another picture of homosexuals is that of the child molester. Child molesters often were themselves molested as children who then fell into the trap of repeating the same patterns, just as adult abusers were often themselves abused. It certainly is not true that all homosexuals are either molesters or abusers.

Female homosexuals, lesbians, are less likely to be part of a gay community than males. Generally, they have more stable relationships than males. Lesbians seem to come from homes where there has been a downplaying of feminine qualities and traditional kinds of play, such as with dolls, and where there has been more competition between mother and daughter, a preference for more active boys games, more of a puritanical attitude towards the body, more shaming of children, or threats and punishment for sex play. Women who have had bad experiences with males— physical, emotional, or sexual abuse—may become lesbians as they develop a caring relationship with another female.

To be more accurate, the majority of lesbians are probably bisexual, engaging in sex with both males and females. By contrast, probably about 30 percent of gays, male homosexuals, are bisexual. Parents whose children "come out of the closet" are often totally surprised because their sons or daughters appeared to exhibit normal interest and dating patterns in the other sex until revealing their homosexuality.

Two other behaviors that need to be mentioned are transsexualism and transvestitism. Transsexuals are people who believe that they are trapped in a body of the wrong sex—really male even though the body is female, or really female even if the body is male. These are the people who will seek sex change operations or seek to pass as a person of the other sex. Often homosexuals who maintain that God creates some as homosexuals will reject the transsexuals as abnormal. Transvestites are people who feel compelled to dress in clothing of the opposite sex. Rather than being sexual in nature, crossdressers often report they do so because it gives them a feeling of power. It is impossible to stereotype who may be a transvestite. Many of them are successfully married and in typically male occupations and yet maintain secret female wardrobes and compulsively cruise in the female clothes in places where nobody knows them. Transvestites may be mistaken for homosexuals because of the stereotype of homosexuals in gay communities wearing bizarre outfits.

Society today supports people who are confused over gender identification and who become homosexual, because of the value placed on being comfortable with one's sexual orientation. The result, I believe, is that many who in the past would have a same-sex experience but would move into more normal behavior are today being convinced that they are gay and are being told that they should accept themselves as gay.

Craig was well-loved by his parents who showed their love for him by buying him "things." His father was caring but distant, very seldom demonstrative either to Craig or his mother. He was often away from home since he maintained long working hours. Craig had a small circle of friends, all of them high-IQ youth like himself who were excluded from the general social scene in high school. He discovered a homosexual community through one of the bulletin boards while telecommunicating on his computer. At first his parents thought his gay friends were simply computer hackers like Craig. By the time they discovered the truth, Craig was firmly entrenched in the gay community, had cast off his religious roots in favor of a church comprised mainly of gays, and was able to refute every theological point that his parents could raise because he no longer accepted Scripture as God's Word authoritative for all time.

Craig became an evangelist for the gay life-style, hoping to convert his parents to what he saw as the correct point of view and openly sneered at the counselor selected by his parents, because he saw the counselor as a person clinging to an antiquated understanding of homosexuality as sin.

Most Resources Available Are Progay

Many parents are confused and dismayed when they start looking for resources to help them talk with a teen about homosexuality and discover that what is available seems to support homosexuality rather than labeling it a sin. I recall a gentleman calling me one day inquiring what our church's stand was on homosexuality. After finding out that we believe it is a sin, he said, "When I was growing up, I learned that this is wrong and that is wrong. Now I'm told that those things are okay. When I talked to my pastor about being gay, he told me that I should be comfortable with who I am because that's the way God made me. You are the first one to tell me that there is such a thing as sin anymore."

Books and pamphlets are available to gays which help them anticipate their parents questions and concerns and counter them. One such pamphlet counsels gays to be patient with their parents since it may take six months to two years before the parents are ready to accept the gay son or daughter. It also counsels that if the gay is living at home or attending college at mom and dad's expense, it may be advisable to wait until they are no longer able to use finances as a club.

There are also many materials available for friends and relatives which are intended to make them feel good about their gay friend/relative and to get them to accept homosexuality as normal behavior. Often parents become confused after being confronted by this material and will compromise their own beliefs in order to establish a good relationship again with their gay son or daughter.

The pro-gay literature will tell you that there is little chance that a person who believes he is gay will ever be straight. Some say that counseling, aversion therapy, behavior modification, and other efforts to change a gay are ineffective with 95 out of 100 gays. Be aware that these figures are talking about individuals who are often exclusively homosexual. Be aware also that materials and programs which claim high success rates are those which work with people who are often bisexual.

What Do I Say to My Teen about Homosexuality?

Don't be an Archie Bunker. Even if the audience agreed with Archie Bunker, most tended to sympathize and support the person he was attacking. The script intentionally made his positions appear narrow minded and out of touch with a society which was passing him by. Archie Bunker was also used to making fun of traditional societal values and religious teachings. It's not just what you say, it's how you say it.

Find out what your teen believes about homosexuality—even if you think you already know. One of my daughters at age 13 thought that homosexuality was perfectly normal and could not understand why they were denied the same rights as recognized minority groups. By the time she was 15, she was disturbed by the thought of homosexuality. Later in her teen years she was deeply troubled by some of the telephone calls from people with gay relatives or people wanting to get out of the gay life. Intended for me, they shared their stories of misery and unhappiness with her when they found out I wasn't home.

Witness to what you believe. Recognize that to moralize against the evils of society often turns a teen off. However, a clear witness to what you believe is not moralizing and often is sought after by your young person (even though you don't realize it). Many young people honestly don't know what their parents believe about important social issues that confront all of us. Therefore they are left to make their own decisions on the basis of other often questionable information available to them. My daughter needed different levels of witness from me depending upon her age, familiarity with the topic, and how well she had processed the information and influences for herself.

Talk about the influences on all of us—teens and adults! Recognize that your teen is being subtly (and not so subtly) influenced to accept homosexuality as normal or alternate behavior. Recognize that all of the media are spattered with progay kinds of presentations.

To ignore the topic of homosexuality is to allow the other forces in society to determine what your teen will believe. Even comic strips in the daily newspaper contain references now to homosexuality—indicating the shift in what we tolerate as acceptable humor for all ages.

Become a discriminating television viewer and talk about what you watch. Watch programs together. Television tends to exploit the latest social issue under the guise of being responsible and contemporary. Feminism, child and spouse abuse, alcohol, drugs—all have been frequent topics. Note how the latest social issue is handled. Observe how gays are presented in TV programs. Is their behavior portrayed as normal? Acceptable? Is the definition of morality presented as practicing safe sex? Is the gay life presented as a happy, care-free life? Or is there an objective presentation of the misery which often accompanies the gay life-style? Is dying of AIDS somehow romanticized? Are objections to homosexuality presented as coming from religious fanatics with an old-fashioned Judeo-Christian ethic? Or is it presented as a violation of behavior acceptable to all people?

Talk about the goodness of God's plan in creating man male and female, how marriage between heterosexuals is what God built into the fiber of all societies. When you affirm the goodness of being male or female and the sanctity of marriage—even though not everybody should or will marry—you are witnessing to what God's plan is for human beings.

Talk specifically about the challenges that your teens face as male or female. Share with them your own struggles when you were a teen. Avoid overemphasizing one aspect of their lives such as excelling in sports, physical attractiveness, or being the most popular person. When you affirm your young people as male or female, let them know they are loved. Help them see how they fit into their own little society and that you are helping them with their own sexual identification and sexual orientation.

What if My Teen Is Gay?

The first thing that you need to do is to stop everything and pray. Don't panic! One writer has said facetiously that you shouldn't say anything to the person for six months. That doesn't mean that you don't talk to each other, but it does mean that you need to be aware of your feelings and careful with what you say.

Normally people who find out about a gay relative are in the grief process the same as with a death or a divorce. There is a real feeling of separation and loss. Remember earlier in the chapter that Craig's parents thought of him as dead! The first stages will be shock, denial, and guilt, before some sense can be made of the situation. You will not go through the stages neatly because circumstances can occur which flip you back and forth. The mother of one gay who came out of the closet in middle age saw her daughter on television blaming her for every bad thing that had ever happened to her in her life. Imagine what a shock that was for her and what it did to her feelings of grief.

Find somebody with whom you can talk. Often parents are afraid to share what they are going through for fear that it will become common knowledge and cause embarrassment and shame for the whole family as well as their gay child. They may not share with their own minister because they believe that it shouldn't have happened, or it hasn't happened to anybody else.

Be concerned about your own welfare and physical, emotional, spiritual well-being. If you are married, be concerned also about your partner. Often husbands and wives become alienated from one another as a result of the pain and the guilt. One woman who said that her marriage was just fine even though they'd found out their daughter was a lesbian also said, "If sex can do this kind of thing to you, I don't want anything to do with it." Claiming to be healthy, she admitted that not a day went by where she did not think about the problem.

If possible, find a support group. We may believe that we are the only ones to be going through the trauma until we notice the many support groups. It is comforting to find other people with the same concerns who can help in the healing process. Unfortunately, in most areas the majority of support groups are pro-gay. But there are groups, especially in urban areas, which help parents work through the grief without simply accepting homosexuality as normal behavior.

One such group is run by Barbara Johnson, whose son was gay. Barbara maintains a listing of groups around the country that offer help to friends and relatives. She can be reached through Spatula Ministries, P.O. Box 444, La Habra, Calif. 90631 (213-691-7369).

You will want to change your gay child. Don't believe that you can change your teen just because you desperately want change. First of all, don't automatically assume that he or she is gay because of coming out of the closet. Get the name of a reputable counselor and establish that the counselor will not simply help your teen accept the fact of being gay. After doing all you can, recognize that you will not change the person nor will a counselor. God changes people, and people are able to be changed if they can recognize the resources they have. Many parents attend a group, go to a counselor, or share with their minister only as long as they think there is a chance that the resource group or person can change the gay. When it doesn't happen, they become bitter and disillusioned and accuse the resource of not really being helpful.

Commit your teen to the Lord. God is powerful and is able to do what we cannot. Many former gays have been changed by clinging to Jesus Christ—some of them after years in the gay community. Frank Worthen, previously mentioned, is director of Love in Action, P.O. Box 2655, San Rafael, Calif. 94912 (415-454-0960). This is a live-in program for males who want to escape the gay life. Frank was first told by his minister that he was gay as a young teenager, became a practicing gay late in his teens, and remained active for a quarter of a century. Frank attributes the success of his program to its strong dependence on God's power.

Continue to pray for your child. Gays often get disturbed when they find out their parents are praying for them. It implies that they are doing something which requires special prayers. But no matter if your teen is actively seeking to change or aggressively attempting to convert you, continue praying that God's will be done and that your child be protected.

Do not compromise your principles and beliefs. Gays often want straight people to be sensitive about their beliefs. You are due the same respect. For example, you have every right to forbid your son from bringing his gay friend to stay for the night just as you would forbid him to sleep with a live-in girl friend in your home. You do him no good by violating what you believe. Don't be deluded into thinking that you are homophobic—afraid of homosexuals—because you cling to God's mandate and power to live a life worthy of who we are in Christ.

Finally, keep communication channels open. Let your son or daughter know your love even though you cannot accept the behavior. Be firm in your witness to what God intends for us as male and female and at the same time clear on the hope that is ours in Jesus Christ.

Remember the words of 1 Cor. 6:9–11: "Do you not know that the wicked will not inherit the kingdom of God? Do not be deceived: Neither the sexually immoral nor idolaters nor adulterers nor male prostitutes nor homosexual offenders nor thieves nor the greedy nor drunkards nor slanderers nor swindlers will inherit the kingdom of God. *And that is what some of you were. But you were washed, you were sanctified, you were justified in the name of the Lord Jesus Christ and by the Spirit of God.*"

Points to Remember

1. Homosexual behavior is promoted in our culture as acceptable behavior.
2. The Bible clearly condemns homosexual behavior as sinful even though attempts are made today to explain away any Scriptural references to homosexuality.
3. There is no clear evidence on why some people become homosexuals. Self-concept, however, is an important factor.
4. Most resources available today on homosexuality are pro-gay.
5. Talk to your teen about what you believe about homosexuality.
6. If your child is gay, don't panic! Pray! Get help!
7. Remember you will go through the bereavement process.
8. Be concerned about your own spiritual welfare as well as the welfare of your teen.
9. Continue to show a wholesome, overt affection for your spouse, especially in the presence of your teen.
10. Commit your teen to the Lord and keep communication channels open.

"No Uncertain Trumpets"

Bob Morrison

*T*he Secretary's office is calling. It's urgent!" That was the message I received late one afternoon last year as I returned to my office in the U.S. Department of Education. The caller was relieved to locate me. She wanted me to help respond to an irate citizen who needed information about youth suicide. Why, the citizen demanded, did not the department have someone assigned to deal with the critical question of suicide among youth? I provided the required answers to the Secretary's assistant. Then I told her, "If you get any more questions like that, tell your questioner that the U.S. Department of Education has a *very* qualified person dealing with youth suicide: Secretary William J. Bennett himself."

Secretary Bennett is highly qualified to deal with the general subject of youth suicide. As one of our country's leading proponents of moral education, he has written extensively on character development among youth. But you, as a Christian parent, are also qualified and can supply a far more basic and important dimension.

Christian parents are qualified by their faith, by their love, and by their intimate knowledge of their own children.

Any parent who has taken a child to a hospital for a mysterious illness will recall the doctor's questioning. A medical history is critically important in determining treatment. That parental knowledge is invaluable in fighting physical ailments. It can be even more important in detecting the often subtle behavioral changes that accompany suicidal thought.

Beyond that, you have much to offer. When the potential of suicide or any other moral problem arises, the Christian parent needs to go back to the very basic fact that laws and mores, on the one hand, do check and control anti-social activity of all people. But, for the Christian, who has been redeemed and is no longer under the threat and punishment of God's law, rules, and mores are guidelines for good living that are followed for the sake of good order and, more important, the Christian observes them as a response to the love of God in Christ. In trying to help teens sort out their problems, this fundmental Biblical truth is basic, a dimension that non-Christian counselors do not understand.

To be qualified does not mean that we are experts in this difficult matter, but merely that we are competent to deal effectively with suicide as it affects our families and those of our friends. Too many parents today have been talked into surrendering their primary authority and responsibility for the well-being of their children. Many experts come to us with impressive credentials, good intentions, and a passionate desire to help, especially in preventing suicide among youth. These experts may seem to "have it all together" with their well-rehearsed and forceful presentations. Their presentations come to us with increasing frequency on radio and television, in newspaper advice columns, or, more recently, in school-based programs. But what these experts don't know is the long history of your family, or that of the Schmidt, Hernandez, or Jones families. Furthermore, the deep commitment the experts have to their cause, while it is highly admirable, cannot compare with the love you have for your child. Dr. James Dobson, the well-regarded psychologist and family counselor, is certainly an expert. But he has underscored this point: You as a parent *are* qualified to cope with your children's problems. You have a God-given authority to direct their education and spiritual growth.

The first and last thing we need to know as parents about suicide is that it is wrong, dead wrong. It is not only wrong for young people, it is wrong for any people. To us as Christians, this may seem to be belaboring the obvious, but it is surprising how little attention is given to this point in the official literature on suicide. The writer who described his science course as teaching him everything about the wasp but why would probably make the same point about some of today's death and dying courses. There our young people can learn everything about suicide but why not. G. K. Chesterton, the Roman Catholic writer, described the act of suicide in these strong terms: "It is not a sin, it is the sin . . . The man who kills a man, kills a man. A man who kills himself kills all men." Chesterton, writing in the early part of this century went on to detail the brutally harsh treatment of suicide during much of the history of Christian Europe. He made it clear that, while he would not commend medieval practices that we would label barbaric, he would use strong words to have us share some of Christianity's historic opposition to the sin of self-killing. St. Augustine said it less dramatically perhaps, but with a sad and sober recognition of the awful nature of the act: "The suicide has done nothing to come into the presence of God."

We begin to defend our children against suicide in a positive way, of course. There is an expression which says that values are more often caught than taught. The value we assign to human life as a gift of God is one which we transmit to our children each day.

The welcome we extend to new members of our families, to new members of our church, and to new neighbors in our community is an example to our children. Our reaction to the death of others is an important model for our children. When a mass killer is executed or when many people are killed in an airplane accident, it is important to react prayerfully and appropriately. The daily, incessant, and often sensationalist media reporting of murder and violence in our world make it all the more important for us to react in a Christian way. Thoreau once wrote that when you had seen one train wreck, you knew about train wrecks. There is much truth in this. Air crash investigators must sift every bit of wreckage of a downed jet liner in order to prevent future accidents, but there seems little reason for the general public to dwell on the morbid details.

"This is the day that the Lord has made. Let us rejoice and be glad in it," the Psalmist writes. This is just one example of the many Biblical injunctions to treasure each day. As we face each day, many of which are fraught with difficulties, stress, occasional conflicts, and sometimes even danger, it's important to show our children that we cherish the gift of life, even when it presents us with challenges.

Direct instruction in our Christian faith is a strong deterrent to suicide among youth. Very young children who know the Lord's Prayer can make applications of such phrases as "Thy will be done," and "Deliver us from evil." Luther's Small Catechism is a rich source of protection, a burnished shield. The commandments teach us not only to fear, love, and trust in God above all things, but to honor our parents and not to kill. Luther's explanation of the Creed contains for us and our children the very core of a pro-life philosophy: "I believe that God has made me and all creatures; that He has given me my body and soul, eyes, ears, and all my members, my reason and all my senses, *and still preserves them* . . . " This is the way Dr. Luther taught us the meaning of the Creed. For young people to memorize these passages and to believe them passionately cannot help but protect them from the evil temptation to commit suicide. A well-established family practice of prayer and fellowship might be regarded as a fire drill routine: most effective when it is rehearsed *in advance of* the danger.

From the beginning of the science of sociology in the nineteenth century, suicide and religion were topics of intense scholarly interest. Emile Durkheim noted that Protestant countries had higher suicide rates (and lower homicide rates) than Catholic countries. He suggested that the greater *communalism* of the Catholic countries and the greater *individualism* of the Protestant countries were a factor in the differing suicide rates. But many modern sociologists have raised doubts about these findings. Sociologist Rodney Stark of the University of Washington sees *connectedness* as a deterrent to suicide, and *isolation* as a factor contributing to it. The mordant humor of the cartoon character who is preparing to take his own life and says, "Good-bye, cruel world," illustrates the point of isolation.

Professor Stark says that active church members are less likely to commit suicide because they are connected; they have many associations which tie them. When all human ties fail, says Stark, there is the Lord. "What a friend we have in Jesus," this scholar maintains, is a powerful statement to the lonely, to those who are otherwise friendless.

So parents who wish to guard their young people against suicide can begin with a firm foundation. They can instruct their children carefully in the Christian faith, they can pray together, they can participate actively in the life of the church.

Communication is always the key to trust in families. Very often the attempted suicide is described as a cry for help. Regular and extensive communication is important to establish the patterns. If family members are accustomed to being reserved and withdrawn from one another, then how can parents determine when their youngsters are becoming *unusually* withdrawn? The teen-age years have always been difficult as young people struggle to establish their own identities. Today parents are sensitive to the increasing potential for danger in alcohol and drug abuse, in pre-marital sex, and even in driving. The teen-age years are a time of changes for parents, too. When young people are more self-reliant, many mothers return to interrupted careers to help prepare for the onset of college tuitions. These devoted mothers may seek to achieve a measure of professional standing after years of selfless service on the home front. They may simply be struggling to keep a roof over the heads of a family where some of the heads seem to be growing a foot taller every year. The increase in the number of female-headed households, where employment outside the home is not an option but a necessity, can also make the teenage years hard ones. These conditions call for special efforts to keep communication channels open. A recent study showed that the average American father spends no more than three minutes a week communicating with his children! Often, tragically, the young suicide is the child of high achieving parents. Fathers should be especially alert to the dangers.

There are ways to compensate for the press of business. Small notes left in lunch bags or on pillows by hurried moms can go a long way to keeping in touch when busy schedules pull families apart. Dads away on required business trips might think to set aside a few minutes to write letters to their teenagers from distant cities. It helps to reduce isolation and to remind your children that, even when you are far away from them, you are holding them close to your heart.

Communication in families can also be helped by regular consultation with pastors, teachers, counselors, principals, and coaches. Pastors and parish lay workers are first stringers on the suicide prevention team. They often see our children in unguarded moments. When communication between children and parents has temporarily snapped, young people frequently turn to their pastors or parish leaders for help. Thank God for these helpers! Many tragic stories are told of model, loving families in which, for one reason or another, barriers have been thrown up against open and honest communication. The young person may have done something—or more likely *thinks* he or she has done something—which will bring shame upon the family. A first brush with the law is often the incident that precipitates the suicide of a model student. To avoid this, pastors and parish youth leaders should be trusted by parents as close, interested, loving helpers who can often overcome barriers to family communication. In studying the literature on youth suicide for two years, and in speaking to many surviving parents of young people who had killed themselves, I never heard of one case of a pastor who claimed to be too busy to help a young person in distress.

Communication with young people is not only important, it is inevitable. If that typical American father communicates with his children only three minutes a week, he can nevertheless be certain that someone else will be taking up the slack. But since American families have been getting smaller with longer intervals between the birth of children, it may not be a trusted older brother or sister who communicates with our youngsters. Increasingly, school, friends, and that odd entity called youth culture have come to dominate the waking hours of our children.

School has changed. For those of us who fondly remember junior and senior high school as a place where trigonometry jitters alternated with the excitement of the pre-game pep rally, the schools of the 80s are a real surprise. In many ways, schools are better equipped to do their jobs than they were in the 50s and 60s. For one thing, there is a genuine commitment to racial equality today which provides the hope of open doors for all. There also has been far greater attention to the educational needs of women—a long overdue improvement. Handicapped persons, too, have been brought into the mainstream. There are many more professionals and para-professionals in today's schools than there were 20–30 years ago. Through the use of multi-media presentations, computer-assisted instruction, and satellite communications, even the remotest schools can participate in the electronic "global village."

Against this hopeful backdrop, however, there have been some disquieting trends. Many public schools and possibly even some parochial schools have offered courses in "values clarification," which all too often suggest that all value choices are equally legitimate and that teachers should not impose their values on students. Chastity and promiscuity, life and death, faith and atheism—each of these has been offered in one guise or another as value choices to be thought out by young people. Of this kind of education it has been said: if we taught dental hygiene the way we teach mental hygiene, our children would have no teeth!

One text widely used in values clarification courses on death and dying is *Problems of Death: Opposing Viewpoints*. David L. Bender, ed. (Minneapolis: Greenhaven, 1981). One of the pamphlets in this text is titled, "Is Suicide Ever Justified?" Four of the seven articles clearly present suicide as a legitimate choice, two articles condemn it, and one simply calls for educating young people about it, without taking a stand. Thus, in the guise of academic freedom, or balance, we have a not too subtle undermining of the entire ethical basis of Western civilization. In many such courses, students engage in morbid activities such as writing their own obituaries, drafting their own living wills, and planning their own funerals. One Florida mother learned only after her son had committed suicide that his science teacher had been describing to the class various ways to poison yourself painlessly! A Richmond, Va. mother learned after her son's suicide that he had been totally wrapped up in the fantasy roleplaying game *Dungeons and Dragons* as part of a so-called gifted and talented school program.

Parents need to know what is going on in their children's public and parochial school classrooms. The vast majority of professional educators are fine, dedicated people, just as the vast majority of the members of the U.S. Navy are patriots and not spies. Interest, knowledge, concern, and involvement with the school will serve to guard against abuses. But never assume that anything done in school must be alright. In particular, be on guard against any school program—be it suicide prevention, drug education, sex education, or social studies—which does not welcome parental involvement.

Despair is sinful, we know, and despair can lead to suicide. Programs in school or on television that suggest the inevitability of an environmental doomsday or a nuclear Armageddon are highly questionable. In an article entitled "Terrorizing Children," two high officials of the U.S. Education Department several years ago condemned many social studies nuclear war units for breeding a radical sense of futurelessness among young people. Chester Finn and Gary Bauer surveyed many school programs to provide evidence of nuclear hysteria. One well-known Australian physician has been giving commencement addresses for years assuring her fresh-faced listeners they have no chance of surviving to age 30. Gloom-and-doom nuclear education is fundamentally dishonest. It fails to explain to young people that at the time the Nazis surrendered in 1945, they still possessed enough deadly nerve gas to kill every man, woman, and child in Britain. We all pray for peace. My family lives less than twenty miles from the White House. I know that if *even one* of the thousands of nuclear weapons now held by hostile powers were dropped on this country, my wife, my children, and I would be killed. I have as much reason as any American to pray for wisdom and strength for the man or woman who occupies the Oval Office. But I will not succumb to nuclear panic. Nor should you. Our hopes and fears as parents are often communicated quite directly to our children. Dr. Robert Coles, the renowned Harvard child psychologist, has written in *The New York Times* that young people who claim to be suffering from nuclear nightmares are really just responding to their parents' hysteria. Thus it is that your Christian faith and your courage can safeguard your children from the temptation to commit suicide because of nuclear nihilism.

Peer pressure is not a new influence among young people, but it is a strong one. The teenage years, strangely enough, are ones of intense group activity and also of intense loneliness. Church programs, athletic teams, after school jobs, and volunteer community service can all be good antidotes to loneliness and idleness. The need for group identity is strong among young people. Unfortunately, Christian young people suffer from ridicule and even harassment in some areas of our country. They need fellowship for mutual support. Recent laws to provide equal access to student religious groups in after-school activities in public schools can help. These rules assure that Christian students will not be made second-class citizens in the schools that their parents' taxes support.

Positive associations for young people stand in marked contrast to the "cluster suicides" that have occurred in such affluent communities as Plano, Tex.; Belleview, Wash.; and Westchester County, N.Y. In those places, students appear to have made suicide pacts and, tragically, to have carried them out. Punk rockers, often from well-to-do suburban homes, are now being seen in many American cities. This unwelcome phenomenon gives evidence of the extraordinarily powerful and pernicious influence of youth peers. Parents need to know who their children's friends are. That is why I cannot urge strongly enough the need to involve your teenagers in the excellent programs of the Missouri Synod's Board of Youth Services. The Lutheran Youth Fellowship should be a vital part in any successful suicide prevention strategy.

"Youthquake" is a coined word sometimes used lightheartedly to describe the vitality and excitement of contemporary youth culture. It is a good word to describe "a whole lotta shakin' goin' on." But parents today need to know how much has changed since we all danced to "Wake up, little Susie." A youthquake, like an earthquake, can describe terrifying tremors rolling across our land, leaving death and devastation in their wake. Recent articles in such prestigious publications as *The Public Interest* and statistics released by the U.S. Department of Education confirm a declining well-being of America's youth. Drug and alcohol abuse have leveled off, but at a very high level. Homicide, fatal traffic accidents, VD, and suicide are at historically high levels. Abortion and AIDS are also bringing grief to many homes. All this has occurred despite more public expenditures than ever on a host of government programs. What has changed? One factor stands out sharply. Our nation has undergone a falling away from the Christian faith. This trend has been particularly bad for young people. From 1952 to 1978, the percentage of young people 18–24 who said religion was very important in their lives plummeted from 64 percent to 37 percent. Weekly church attendance for the under-30 age group dropped from 48 percent in 1958 to 29 percent in 1977. There are, of course, some recent hopeful signs of a renewed religious commitment among youth, but the figures above show that we must work to bring millions of young people back into the church.

Another change over the past 30 years has been the degradation of youth culture in films and music. "Meet Buddy, 360 pounds of CLEAVERMANIA and he's going hog wild!" reads the large ad in *The Washington Post*. The prestigious newspaper advertises a movie called *Slaughterhouse*. Although rated "R," this film is clearly directed toward the lucrative youth market. Many of these young people are in the 17–24 age bracket. They have money, are not excluded from movie theaters showing "R" rated films, and perhaps not coincidentally have a very high rate of suicide. How closely will neighborhood theaters check IDs? How hard will video store owners work to keep "Buddy" out of the hands of minors? When was the last time you or any adult you know hurried to see such a film as *Slaughterhouse?* Clearly, ambitious producers and distributors of such stomach-turning products—which often feature murder and human dismemberment as fit subjects for entertainment—have a target audience in mind. Their target is your children.

Recent hearings on Capitol Hill made millions of Americans aware for the first time of a thing called "Porn Rock." The extent of the obscenity and gross violence contained in records and tapes shocked many of us. Adults are inclined to view this aspect of youth culture with a bemused and detached tolerance, rather like the grandmother in the TV ad who smiles sweetly as her punk rocker grandson goes by. He's just given her a "pick me up" bouquet, but his choice of music may drive him to the grave before his grandmother. The sad fact is some of the most respected and powerful corporations in the United States are profiting from music which promotes violence, perverted sex, drug use, occultism, hatred of women, and suicide.

The Smithsonian Institution, surely one of the most popular attractions in our nation's capital, gave testimony to the popularity of the movie and TV series "M*A*S*H" when it enshrined the show's costumes and sets. The show is well-known for its irreverent brand of humor. Religion and marriage are routinely ridiculed. This, one is reminded, is a *very* free country. But the musical theme of "M*A*S*H" goes too far. The first verse reads: "Suicide is painless, it brings on many changes. And I can take or leave it if I choose." Not much, unfortunately, can be expected from the crew who gave us a parody of the Last Supper played as a suicide plot in the original film version. It is small wonder that Dr. Dobson, one of the kindliest men in public life today, said he *hated* "M*A*S*H."

Thankfully, many parents and their teens are banding together to do something about porn rock. The Parents Music Resource Center (PMRC) has led the way in exposing the dangers. Patterned on the very successful Mothers Against Drunk Driving (MADD) group, PMRC has offered parents, students, and church groups a rich source of documentation of lyrics and record album cover graphics. Though the group strenuously avoids censorship, their work makes it possible for parents to be forewarned and forearmed. PMRC informs us that a prominent rock star is being sued by the parents of a young suicide who shot himself while listening to an unlovely song called "Suicide Solution." Parents Music Resource Center can be reached at PMRC, Suite 350, 1500 Arlington Blvd, Arlington, Vir. 22209 (703-527-9466). Because many groups like these have been formed, the social acceptability of the targeted activities has been lessened.

MADD is not seen, perhaps, as a specifically anti-suicide group. Nonetheless, we know that alcohol abuse is strongly correlated with youth suicide. Also, many of the vehicular deaths of young people are what Dr. David Phillips of the University of California at San Diego calls disguised suicides. Therefore, success against alcohol abuse among young people will work against suicide.

Similarly, the national attention given to the "Just Say NO" campaign against drugs is bound to help. Drugs, in addition to causing dangerous physical and psychological addiction, have been seriously implicated in youth suicide. Many drugs act as depressants and can induce those mental states often associated with suicide. Because drugs are illegal, dosages are inexact. Many young people may lose their lives to unintentional overdoses. As with car wrecks, others may simply choose this method of ending their lives without leaving evidence of suicidal intent.

The important point for parents is this: Drugs, alcohol, and reckless driving are all suicide indicators. By acting against these forms of abuse, we communicate to our young people a strong sense of the value we place on their lives. We show that we disapprove most strongly of life-threatening behaviors. Parents can seek help from pastors, counselors, school officials, and law enforcement authorities; it's what has been called "tough love" and it's working.

As in almost any human endeavor, there are different schools of thought in the suicide prevention field. Some of the respected professionals seek to demystify death, to discuss suicide openly with young people, to destigmatize the act of suicide in our culture. All this is done in a well-intended effort to eliminate suicide among youth. "Talking about it can't hurt," these professionals often say. As a result of this view, these suicidologists often seek aggressively to place programs within public schools and some parochial schools. Legislation in Congress now would provide federal funds for model programs to place courses on suicide prevention in selected schools.

Another view on suicide prevention, however, says that not enough is known about such crucial issues as contagion and suggestibility. Until we do know these facts, these activists say, the safest rule of thumb is "Above all, do no harm." Many of these participants in the debate prefer that no mention of suicide be made while teaching impressionable young people.

Christians are admirably equipped to cope with the broad outlines of this problem. Our understanding of Law and Gospel prepares us. We have no hesitation, on the one hand, in condemning the *act* of suicide and doing everything we can to prevent it while, on the other hand, asserting that God loves all sinners with a love that is powerful enough to overcome even death.

In faith, we can approach this problem with Christian realism. To attempt to banish any mention of the word suicide is unrealistic. It is not unlike the fairy tale, "Sleeping Beauty." The royal parents tried to destroy all the spinning wheels in the kingdom lest their beloved daughter prick her finger on one and die. But the "professionals" who seek to bombard young people with all the facts of suicide haven't quite got it right either. Their approach—like TV's Sergeant Friday—"just the facts, ma'am"—ignores the most important facts of Christian faith and love. The real solution to youth suicide, I suggest, is to encourage young people to contemplate not guns and ropes and gasses, but the cross of Jesus Christ.

My own view of suicide was first formed by my experience in the Coast Guard. "You *have* to go out," was the motto. It meant that saving lives in peril on the sea was a duty so plain and so obvious, that there could be no debate. When we were taught to be lookouts on board ship, we were instructed *not* to look directly for the man in the water. If you want to find a shipwrecked person, they told us, lift up your sights. There is a very good scientific reason for this: The cones and rods in the eye function in such a way at night that they can best pick up a figure in the water by not looking directly at it.

In a similar way, I think we Christians can face the problem of suicide if we first lift up our sights to the Lord. Then we can use all the scientific and social research and the excellent resources of modern service agencies. We will have a framework in which we can employ all the tools we need. The Christian home, as we understand it, comprised of faithful and loving family members, may prove to be the best defense against the scourge of youth suicide. For such families, we all pray.

Points to Remember

1. The value we place on human life is transmitted to our children each day.
2. Leading an active Christian life is a strong deterrent to suicide among youth.
3. Communication is a key factor in establishing trust among family members.
4. Parents need to know what is being taught in their school classrooms and be involved in the educational process.
5. Any program which stresses positive values for youth will also help as a preventive against teenage suicide.
6. A strong Christian home may prove to be the best defense against youth suicide.

Healthy Sexuality vs. "Safe" Sex

Howard Mueller

𝒯he sexual revolution of the past quarter century is over, a national news magazine concluded early in 1987. For the presumed freedom and casual pleasure it brought, followers of the revolution paid a high price: unwanted pregnancies, 4,000 abortions a day, broken hearts and homes, sex instead of sexuality, one night stands instead of friendships. Yet none of these seriously challenged the revolution. But now a virus whose stealthy partner is death has decreed the revolution's end.

"I can't emphasize too strongly the necessity of changing lifestyles," Dr. Otis R. Bowen, secretary for Health and Human Services, has declared.

The social issue of sexually transmitted disease (STD) is a life and death challenge to the home, church, and society. The current situation is this: AIDS is primarily a sexually transmitted disease, although infected mothers can give the disease to their infants. AIDS is the acronym for Acquired Immune Deficiency Syndrome. Current usage prefers the designation HIV, Human Immunodeficiency Virus. Both refer to the fact that this virus attacks the immune system, the marvelous system that protects us against invading viruses, bacteria, and cells which are not compatible with our own healthy cells. The immune system is permanently neutralized; the power to resist disease is gone forever. Normally, the viruses of common colds and other diseases temporarily overpower the immune system, but with time and rest the immune system prevails, and the patient recovers.

An immune system permanently shut down is not in itself fatal. People do not die directly of AIDS. In fact, they do not even know that they have contracted it because the HIV organism can lie dormant in the human system for as long as eight years. During this time infected individuals feel no ill effects, nor do they know without testing that they are hosts to the virus. Once the virus becomes active, the inoperative immune system renders the AIDS victim helpless to all the viruses and bacteria that can cause disease. Even before individuals know that they have AIDS, they can unintentionally pass the virus on to sexual partners.

After less than 10 years' experience with AIDS it is not yet known how many infected persons will contract fatal opportunistic diseases—illnesses which take advantage of the immune system's helplessness against them. Two are particularly common: Pneumoncystis carinii, a form of pneumonia which in progressively more debilitating attacks drains life strength, and Kaposi's sarcoma, a cancer that appears on body surfaces, first as brownish or purplish spots, then as ulcerating sores. These patients diagnosed as having AIDS are highly susceptible to tuberculosis. Other venereal disease, if present, does not respond successfully to treatment. Additional grave manifestations of illness include weight loss of one-third of body weight, extreme weakness signaling the disintegration of life itself and severe pain. Loss of control over eliminative functions is common. In over 30 percent of the infected persons the HIV virus travels directly to the brain with disastrous consequences: loss of memory. impaired judgment and, in the final stages, loss of intellectual function not unlike Alzheimer's disease. During the final months the sufferer is totally helpless and dependent on others.

Unless treated with AZT, death comes normally within two years after the person becomes ill.

By 1991 America will have had 270,000 active cases of AIDS, and 5 to 10 million persons will be carriers of the virus. Blacks and Hispanics are disproportionately affected, having a 25 percent higher infection rate than the white population. It is probable that by the time the epidemic has run its course each one of us will have mourned the death of a child, a sister, a brother, or a friend who has died of AIDS.

The cost of medical care for an AIDS infected person for the period of illness can run $40,000—$150,000, according to an estimate by the president of the American Medical Association. A person who becomes ill sooner or later will lose his job and with it his medical benefits. Public programs do not exist outside a few local communities. The sick are dependent on family and friends. Families of modest means have mortgaged their homes in order to provide care for an afflicted son or daughter. In most cases the family home and resources are endangered if a family member comes down with illness following HIV infection.

While AIDS is the ultimate venereal scourge, it is not the only one. Sexually transmitted diseases, affecting primarily persons 17–35 years, make up the largest group of infectious diseases in the world. After a decline in syphilis and gonorrhea early in the 1980s, the incidence of these diseases has risen again among sexually active persons. Though these diseases are treatable, youth are at special risk because ignorance of symptoms, embarrassment, ignorance of treatment availability, and lack of resources to seek and pay for treatment permit untreated infections to run rampant.

Gonorrhea causes painful infections of the reproductive organs and the urinary tracts in both males and females. In women the infection can cause scarring of the fallopian tubes and subsequent sterility. If the infection spreads, a gonococcal arthritis can result. Infants passing through an infected birth canal can contract an eye infection.

Persons aged 20–24 show the highest incidence of syphilis. First stage syphilis presents itself in the form of a chancre at the site of infection. This can be the genitals, lips, female breasts or mouth. Secondary syphilis follows six to eight weeks later with eruptions on the palms, soles and mucous membranes. Other symptoms may appear, such as sore throat, mild upper respiratory infection, and general lethargy. The disease can be transmitted from mother to fetus. Late stage syphilis can affect the heart 10 to 25 years after the initial infection, significantly impairing the length and quality of life. Neurosyphilis surfaces in persons in their 40s and 50s. Behavior changes, irritability, memory loss, poor judgment, headaches, and insomnia are initial signs that can progress to the point that a person is shabby, unkempt, exhibits emotional irritability, depression, and delusions of grandeur. The sexually transmitted diseases—we haven't described all of them—exact a tragic price of suffering, life-shortening, and debilitating illness, climaxing in death. It is largely youth in the freshness and promise of their first adult years who pay the price.

What makes the threat of AIDS a priority concern is the present fear of medical scientists that youth are the next targeted group to be seriously affected by AIDS. Dr. Harold Jaffe, chief epidemiologist in the AIDS program at the Centers for Disease Control, has said: "Teenagers potentially are a problem group for AIDS." His concerns are well founded.

Despite the need for preventive sex education, parents, churches, schools, and health departments have not given education the priority it must have. Some critics of sex education blame education itself for being responsible for spreading concepts of promiscuous sex and actually thus increasing the incidence of sexually transmitted diseases. Certainly, there are programs which do promote values inconsistent with our Christian faith, but that is all the more reason to provide solid programs through homes and churches.

A major problem is that teenagers often feel invulnerable. Enjoying the vibrant energies of youth, they find death beyond their intellectual grasp, unless they've somehow experienced death firsthand. They strongly deny that anything can cause them to lose their health or kill them.

Significant numbers of youth are engaging in activities known to put them at high risk of HIV infection. More than 11.6 million teens (80% of the boys and 70% of the girls) between the ages of 13 and 19 years have engaged in sexual intercourse. One in seven adolescents has had a sexually transmitted disease. One million teenage girls become pregnant each year. No one knows how many carriers are teens, but their number is growing. When they find out in their 20s, it will be too late for them and for the partners they had in their adolescent years.

HIV infection cannot be predicted from every sexual encounter, but neither can freedom from infection. Chemical abuse can heighten the risk by stressing the immune system, and a stressed immune system is more vulnerable to HIV infection. Many youth have their first and later sexual encounters while intoxicated. Marijuana, cigarette smoking, and cocaine stress the immune system and create conditions favorable to irreversible HIV infection.

With deadly stealth the AIDS virus is encroaching on our homes and all individuals, from youth through adults. There is no defense, save one. Scientific medicine has worked heroically to identify the HIV agent and learn its mode of transmission. It has succeeded only in discovering that this virus is different from any they have seen before. They have no medicine that overpowers the virus nor a vaccine that can prevent its attack on the immune system. The most optimistic projections of an effective vaccine place its availability into the mid-1990s, too late to be of any help to the youth of today.

The one effective defense against AIDS is in our hands. Dr. C. Everett Koop, surgeon general of the United States, has said repeatedly that our first medical defense is abstinence or a commitment to a monogamous relationship with one uninfected person. For the Christian that relationship describes marriage.

The sexual revolution is over

But its momentum is not. Sexual practices incorporated into the fabric of American life for over a generation will not capitulate easily.

If you think that AIDS, terrible as it is, is a scourge remote from your life and not likely to affect the young person whom you love, now is the time to come face-to-face with the truth.

If you have hoped that the young woman or young man in your home would pass through the teen years unscarred by the sexual revolution, now is the time to open your eyes to the risks and the facts.

You have a task as urgent as saving a life

Some adults are almost paralyzed by the thought of speaking about sex and the sexual life with their children. Where does one start? Where does one find language through which to express oneself? How can we speak of an aspect of life so intimate that mention of it is avoided, even in the physician's examining room? These barriers must be overcome. With the arrival of AIDS, we are finally realizing that silence comes at too high a price. Fortunately, a sensitive manual is available. Written by Lenore Buth, *How to Talk Confidently with Your Child about Sex* (previously titled *Sexuality: God's Precious Gift to Parents and Children*) speaks clearly, openly, and winsomely about sex and sexuality. Every Christian parent should read and absorb this book to gain confidence. Be thoroughly prepared before you speak. Only silence between a parent and an adolescent is worse than a single brief conversation. Open, frank, and natural education in the home is the nation's first and best defense against AIDS.

Another potential source of self-consciousness and hesitation can be your own sexual past. A mother sat next to the bed of her sleeping daughter in the maternity section, weeping softly. Earlier that day her daughter had delivered a stillborn child. As a chaplain approached, the mother in her upper forties said: "This is my punishment for a misstep I made when I was her age." After a quarter century into the sex revolution, numbers of parents are still guilt-ridden by events in their earlier years that they would rather forget, but forgetting does not satisfy conscience. Speaking to youth about sexuality and sexual ideals, they hear a voice within that challenges their right to speak. Yet as forgiven people made clean by the blood of Jesus Christ and as repentant sinners, they do possess the right and obligation to speak to their teens. A forgiven adult brings a realism, a humility, and a personal commitment to conversations with youth about what it means to live as one of God's holy people in a world where it seems "everybody is doing it." Youth can spot the symptoms when an adult is uncomfortable with a topic or feels unsure about it.

Fortunately, a parent's convincing present behavior makes a deeper impression on youth than a past life-style that contradicted it. Young people are highly perceptive of parents' present submission to the Holy Spirit in their sexuality. In the Christian life the past is reversible. A Christian family is built on the reconciling fact of life in Jesus Christ.

Think of the 13- to 15-year-old male and female in our society and all of the different circumstances in which they may be growing up: two-parent family, first marriage; two-parent family, second marriage; single-parent family, never married; single-parent family, previously married, now widowed, divorced, or separated; parent(s) living together unmarried; and adoptive families. Many of these family forms may reflect guilt feelings over past sins or current living situations.

Complicate this by the fact that teens look to adults as authority figures—even though it may not seem to be so—and realize that youth are confronted with many different life-styles as they are developing their own understandings of life. As they see the authority models and perhaps even challenge them, they develop their own internalized set of values. Young people need parental direction from mature adults who have internalized their own values, goals, and decision-making processes. Adolescents stand at a transition point, which under normal conditions can take five years or more. Meanwhile, they will overreach themselves, wanting more decision-making power than they can handle. Parents often feel more secure with the way it was when their children were small and their authority went unquestioned and now become anxious that youth are asking for more than they can capably manage. This seesaw struggle produces much tension in homes and directly determines how your family deals with AIDS and other sexually transmitted diseases.

In his 1986 report to the Carnegie Corporation, corporation president David Hamburg said:

"While the human organism is reproductively mature in early adolescence, the brain does not reach a fully adult state of development until the end of the teenage years, and social maturity lags well behind. Young adolescents, aged 10–15, are able to and do make fateful decisions that affect the entire life course, even though they are immature in cognitive development, knowledge, and social experience. Their need for knowledge and guidance in making choices and becoming effective social beings rests clearly with their parents."

Young people go through stages. At times relationships with the other sex seem to consume all their energy, and at other times the sexual questions seem to be lying dormant. Parents can respond to both stages as they recognize them, responding to each set of issues raised. When there is interest in the other sex, issues about sexuality can be addressed. When they are not surface issues, it is still important to model what it means to be male or female, to stress the sanctity of marriage and the principles that underlie relationships between the sexes.

Puberty introduces a new stage of sex education. Hormonal changes in a comparatively short time will produce the most startling changes a human being experiences after birth. Wide mood swings, erratic judgment, and uncertainty about self accompany the changes. A girl takes on a female figure, her eyes sparkle with new life, and she experiences menstruation. She needs your assurance again and again that she is attractive. A boy will experience penile erections, nocturnal emissions, a changed voice and the growth of facial hair. He needs an explanation of what is happening to him and the reassurance that it's a normal part of his developing manhood. Sex is the strong new factor in the life of youth. It takes a priority consistent with its transforming effect.

What forms of expression will it take? Today's society facilitates the physical expression of sex. Peers confer a special aura on those known to engage in sex. Television is often milder than movies, but both graphically portray sex, and both ultimately end up on the television screen through networks, cable, or VCRs. The courts, granting youth access to contraceptive information and technology, and to abortions without parental consent, have given them almost complete freedom of choice in their sexual life and have established sex between consenting adults as normal behavior. Critics of the unrestricted freedom in sexual matters which tempts and tantalizes youth rightly point out that an adolescent can readily obtain birth control pills while at the same time needing a note from parents to be given aspirins.

This is more responsibility than many adolescents can handle and directly violates their consciences and belief systems. The other side of the coin is that any youth today can find other youth who will proclaim the theme that chastity is outmoded and casual sex the only pattern worthy of an enlightened society.

How then do we deal with the current threat of loose morals, easy sex, and the resulting life-threatening diseases? The majority of information presented thus far in this chapter has been negative. Yet it must be presented to both youth and adults. AIDS has been used to scare people into responsible behavior that is also in accord with God's will and with the requirements for a decent society. All of us need to be aware of the threats to us as individuals, families, and as a society. We need the facts which explain sexually transmitted diseases and their consequences, including AIDS. It must be known that the transmission of AIDS follows a pattern that sex with one partner links those partners with every other sexual partner that each of them has had.

Safe sex is promoted as a relatively reliable way to continue with sexual partners and avoid the possibilities of contracting sexually transmitted disease. The idea of safe sex—if there really could be such—flaunts the standards which God specifically condemns. God forbids fornication (sex between unmarried) and adultery (sex with the spouse of another). Opponents of maintaining sexual standards claim that sexual abstinence is an outmoded way of life clung to by religious fanatics.

There is a serious difference between the proponents of safe sex and those who claim that sex is to be expressed only within the bonds of marriage. The safe sex advocates either believe that it is impossible to get people to be sexually chaste and therefore we must face the reality of the situation or believe that sexual chastity inhibits full human expression. The chastity advocates fall into several camps also. On one side may be those who see all sex as evil and on the other side those who see it as a good gift of God to be expressed in the God-pleasing estate of marriage.

The role of government is also viewed variously. Some believe that the government should do all that it can to find a cure for AIDS so that people can continue to be sexually free from consequences of their actions. Others certainly want to find a cure but believe that government should be promoting morality rather than safe sex alternatives.

All of this is confusing to both youth and adults. Combine this with the confusion over exactly how AIDS can be contracted together with the seeming disregard among many youth for the personal threat to them as individuals, and it may cause you to throw up your hands in despair and wonder what you can actually do.

Specific Suggestions for Talking to Your Teens

Anticipate the accusation: "You don't trust me." Plan your answer. Responses could include "Is that the message I'm giving? . . . I love you; it's the world out there I don't trust. . . . I also don't want you put into situations which you can't handle. I thought I was giving you information: you will face the decisions when I'm not there. . . . You have been born into a world which knows few sexual restraints and now AIDS is forcing a radical change in that world. . . . There are terrible pressures on adults, too. I have to make decisions, much as that may surprise you. . . . We all need to live defensively. . . . God gives me a responsibility for you which I gladly accept as an adult. . . ."

But giving information and advice and warnings are not enough. Youth need specific responses to specific situations. Many of the programs modeled after "The Just Say No" campaigns stress actual roleplaying so that the young people get experience talking through decisions which, while perhaps uncomfortable, may actually get to feel natural. You can make a game out of it in your home as you roleplay potentially compromising situations: parties where liquor is used, an invitation to a youth's home whose parents are not there; advances which strongly imply that sex will follow. Let them formulate their decisions in language which they can understand and accept.

The teen years are a time to develop heterosexual skills: the abilities necessary to get along with persons of both sexes and to function in a world which increasingly offers opportunites for both sexes. At the same time there is such an emphasis on physical sex in the society and among teenagers that healthy sexual development can be thwarted by the focuses of society. Recall again the teen sex-movies made specially for the teenage group which is supposed to be too young to attend them! Attention to continued healthy growth of the body—education, the development of special gifts received from God, movement toward a career choice—these, too, are the exhilarating tasks of youth. Each facet of these expanding promises needs proportional concentration. A tendency of youth (or parents) to focus on one to the exclusion of the rest gives adults the opportunity to help youth maintain balance and move toward healthful maturation.

An important task as parent is to be a model for youth. That's an important reason why you need to work through your own sins and shortcomings and recognize the forgiveness that is yours through Jesus Christ. Realizing who you are, you can nurture your teens in their sexuality, affirm them, and watch them grow physically, emotionally, and spiritually. You can thrill to the pleasure of being a living model of a Christian male or female. Then, when your daughter feels a rush of excitement each time a certain youth at school looks at her, or your son can't take his eyes off a girl in the youth group, the chances are good that they will talk their feelings over with you.

The peer group—its music, language, dress, and preferred activities—will take on an authority that may frighten you. But if your youth are still sharing concerns with you, chances are that you are still a powerful influence. You may hear, "Everybody does it" and accept it as a complaint against friends instead of a justification of actions. Listen to all that your youth are willing to share and toss your way. Continue to witness to what you believe rather than simply be quiet, or react negatively.

You may come to the conviction that the peer group with which your youth associate is not socially healthy. Raise your objections but not without hearing their side and affirming their right to identify with a group. Talk through your concerns. Consider options for more productive associations. Remember that out of loyalty youth may defend people and conduct which they don't really approve. Be patient, and if the peer group is an unhealthy one, consider getting outside help from professionals or even your youth's other peers. Assist your daughter or son in the search for new friends or a peer group, and accept persons from the new peer group warmly.

Physical sex by adolescents tends to impoverish other social relationships, just as casual sex outside of marriage will break up the adult group. The peer group which will be most meaningful is one which develops around friendship, a spirit of sharing, a commonality of values, and even experiencing the joys and frustrations of going through the various stages of life. It will not be held together by fears such as the fear of AIDS. The positive qualities of commitment, cooperation, friendship, and a recognition of God as Creator and His Son as Redeemer will do more to motivate than any false motivators based on fear.

In dealing with the healthy development of sexuality and social relations of youth, be aware that the transitional experience may be sufficiently difficult to warrant professional help. Warning signs include: severe distress meeting youth socialization demands; sexual behavior threatening to get out of control; religious and moral value systems that seem ineffective; indecision or confusion about a career; badly faltering academic performance; and little or no evidence of loyalty to family, church, or school. If these conditions persist without modification for three months or longer, consult a counselor experienced in adolescent problems. Untreated, he or she may suffer a great deal of emotional pain, begin to act out sexually and take an unfortunate turn in life that isn't necessary.

Your home atmosphere will ultimately help to determine how much at risk or strong your youth will be when the sexual revolution confronts them. Pornography, sex-saturated entertainment, sex crimes, and sex humor dominate our culture. Is your home open to them, or do you maintain moral standards which screen out immorality? The popularity of a show cannot be an admission ticket to the Christian home. Your reading and entertainment choices should be consistent with the healthy sexuality to which you are pledged. The absence of entertainment standards conditions all of us to become a part of the sex revolution, as little as we want that and as lethal to our welfare as such a decision may be.

The devotional life of your home can supply youth with another tool for developing inner strength to cope with the world. Excuses of a lack of time or know-how for devotional life usually point beyond themselves to a deeper problem: We are uncomfortable sharing ourselves, our witness to the love of Christ within us, our spiritual needs and struggles, even though they are quite apparent to those who know us well. We become self-conscious when others share themselves, share Christ, share their struggles with us. However, too much is at stake for ourselves, our children, and our youth not to risk self-disclosure.

The Scriptures offer some memorable occasions when healthy sexuality was reinforced or undermined. An adult discussion of Joseph and Potiphar instead of the primary grade Sunday school presentation could be an eye-opener as you look at Potiphar's wife who made adulterous sexual advances to Joseph (Gen. 39:6–10). You can discover a strong model of God-fearing integrity in Joseph. When another Joseph found the devout young woman whom he loved and admired pregnant, his natural conclusion was that Mary had succumbed to casual sex (Matt. 1:18–22). You can contrast vividly what the cost of recreational sex would be to your ideals of womanly sexuality and the loss of respect and esteem of persons who value her womanhood. In each example, God is the key to the decision. With a little ingenuity, other Bible events that illuminate some facet of sexuality can tell their story and challenge modern youth.

The key to talking to youth about AIDS and other sexually transmitted diseases is not that you become an expert in the literature and are able to expound the latest theory on causes, the latest statistics on numbers of cases, and all of the arguments pro and con about the sexual revolution. The key is that you know who you are as a child of God, redeemed by Jesus Christ; that you know what it means to be a parent in today's world; and that you are able to witness to who you are and who your youth can be—also in Christ.

Talking to teens about AIDS is really no different from talking about any other life issue! The issues will continue to come up, but God offers us strength which is more than sufficient.

"The one who sows to please his sinful nature, from that nature will reap destruction; the one who sows to please the Spirit, from the Spirit will reap eternal life. Let us not become weary in doing good, for at the proper time we will reap a harvest if we do not give up. Therefore, as we have opportunity, let us do good to all people, especially to those who belong to the family of believers" (Gal. 6:8–10).

In spite of all the negatives around us, when we exhibit that which is God pleasing, we do a good work anchored in Him!

Points to Remember

1. Open, frank, and natural education in the home is the nation's first and best defense against AIDS.
2. Teens look to adults as authority figures—even though it may not seem so.
3. The idea of safe sex flaunts the standards which God specifically condemns.
4. If a youth shares concerns with a parent, that means that the parent still is a powerful influence.
5. The key to talking to youth about AIDS and sexually transmitted diseases is not in being an expert in the subject but is in knowing self as a forgiven child of God, redeemed by Jesus Christ.
6. Talking about AIDS is really no different than talking about other issues.
7. The best defense is a good offense built around a home where Jesus Christ is central!

My Kid on Drugs—Never!

Ed Eggert

*I*t can't be! It just CANNOT be!'' That's the conviction of many parents today when first facing the reality that their adolescent son or daughter is "into drugs." The denial syndrome is as strong or even stronger on the part of many parents as it is in the adolescent. Consequently, parents don't recognize the attitudinal and behavioral changes in their child. Early indications of drug use are ignored, minimized, or rationalized as just a teenage phase. A curfew is broken, your previously pleasant child begins to snip back at you; there are more and more heated arguments, less and less chit-chat about school, sports, or friends; their plans—where they are going or where they have been—become more vague. They seem to be becoming more secretive about whom they are talking to on the phone. You begin to notice less and less interest in school and homework. Now, when they do come home, they go directly to their rooms and come out only for specific chores or mealtime.

Then one day you get a call from the school guidance counselor, inquiring about your child's health. He or she has not been in school that day, in fact there have been a number of absences during the past few weeks. You are not only surprised, you are convinced there is an error some place, because you know your child went to school every day. The counselor invites you to come to his office, so that together you might resolve the "error."

When you meet with the counselor, he not only shows you your child's poor attendance record, but also informs you that your child, who had been an excellent student with A's and B's for the first marking period, now has several D's and one incomplete. You are shocked, embarrassed, bewildered, searching desperately for a logical explanation. The counselor tries to relieve some of your pain, and together, you begin to compare notes. Somewhere in that exchange, the counselor raises the question as to the possibility of drug use. Your first reaction is, "It can't be, not my child." But as the counselor reviews the signs and symptoms of drug use or abuse, you slowly begin to recognize some of these same attitudes and behavior in your own child.

What I have described so far are *early* signs and symptoms of chemical abuse. Chemical dependence being a progressive illness, we see the severity of problems increase. The abuse of chemicals destroys relationships. Communication with you, the parent, with brothers and sisters, or previous nonusing friends, deteriorates. There is an onset of legal problems such as truancy, shoplifting, stealing money from the home or other items which can be easily pawned, driving under the influence or without a license, assault and battery, resisting arrest, minor in possession, or being picked up as a "runaway."

There may also be emotional and more bizarre behavioral changes, such as depression, thoughts of or attempts at suicide, agitation and impulsiveness, paranoia, and temporary loss of memory.

Chemical dependence has physical, emotional, and spiritual ramifications. This is true also of the adolescent.

Since I have used the term *chemical dependence* rather than alcoholism or drug addiction, I feel I should explain. In the 1940s and 1950s, when people talked about an *addiction*, more often than not, the reference was to alcohol addiction. We spoke of the *alcoholic*. Gradually, we began to recognize another, namely, drug addiction. When we first spoke of *drug addicts*, we referred to people using *narcotics* such as morphine, codeine, demoral, dilaudid; or *sedatives* such as quaaludes, barbiturates, such as phenobarbital, nembutal, or seconal; *tranquilizers* such as librium, valium, tranzene or dalmane; *stimulants* such as amphetamines such as ritalin, benzedrine, dexedrine, speed. In many circles these two addictions, namely, alcohol and drug addiction, were viewed as two totally different addictions. In recent years we have seen more and more dual addiction, that is, the same person addicted to alcohol plus any or several of the other mood-altering drugs I have just referred to.

We have also learned that if a person who is addicted to either the drug or the alcohol, (alcohol too is a drug—under the category of sedatives) chooses to give up the one and substitutes the other, almost without exception, he or she will become addicted to the substitute rather quickly and in most instances will revert to the original "drug of choice." Today, we see very few people coming into treatment centers using only one drug. Invariably, they are abusing alcohol plus any number of other drugs. This is true also of adolescents. Frequently abused drugs among the adolescents are alcohol, pot, speed, cocaine, acid, or as I frequently hear, "Whatever is available." Therefore, instead of referring to alcoholics or drug addicts, thinking of them as two totally different addicts, we refer to them today as *chemically dependent*, denoting a *dual dependence*.

I need to go back now and add a few more comments about the signs and symptoms as well as the progression of the illness. Please refer to the chart "The Disease of Chemical Dependency in Adolescence." In reading the chart, begin in the upper left hand corner and read down. As you read the indicators in the *early, crucial, and chronic phase*, you will note a number of black dots. Each one of these marks a crucial step in the progression of the illness. As in any other illness, the earlier treatment or intervention occurs, the greater the potential for restoration to health. This is equally true in chemical dependence. The earlier the intervention, the greater the potential for recovery. I will say more about *intervention* later.

The chart entitled, "Levels of Alcohol Use" is designed to let you see from another perspective the progression from *use* to *dependency*. Here is yet another visual perception of the stages of chemical abuse:

Nonuse: No life problems
Use: Possible consequences

Misuse: Possible consequences—the potential for harm or other problems

Abuse: Serious life problems. Can document negative affect—miss school; home, legal, driving problems.

Dependency: Multiple life problems. Truly out of control. Preoccupation with alcohol and/or drugs.

The signs and symptoms and the progression scale is virtually the same, regardless of the drug of choice. We do see some change in the period of time from misuse to dependence—depending on the number of different drugs being misused. This also helps us to understand how youngsters 13, 14, or 15 years of age can be diagnosed as being "chemically dependent."

A generally accepted time frame for an adult, from the onset of misuse of alcohol to the point of addiction (being physically and emotionally dependent) is about 8 to 10 years. If that were true of the 13-, 14-, or 15-year-old adolescent, he or she would have to misuse alcohol at age 3, 4, or 5, which would be highly unlikely. However, as stated earlier, rarely do we see an adolescent in a treatment center who hasn't misused anywhere from three to six or more drugs, simultaneously.

When a number of mood-altering drugs are used such as alcohol, pot, speed, cocaine, or acid—some of those more commonly used by adolescents—a *synergistic* reaction takes place. To use a mathematical example: If I drink two parts of alcohol and add two parts of another mood-altering drug, I would expect a reaction equal to four parts. However, as a result of the *synergistic* reaction the effect would be quite different. *Synergistic* is defined as "the simultaneous action of separate agencies [any two or more mood-altering drugs] which together have greater total effect than the sum of their individual effect" (Webster's New World Dictionary). What this means is that two or more parts of one drug taken with two or more parts of another drug, does not equal four, but could have the effect of 8, 16, 32 or more parts.

Another term frequently used is that one drug *potentiates* the effect of the other, that is, "to increase or multiply the effect of a drug or toxin by the preceding or simultaneous administration of another drug or toxin" (Webster's New World Dictionary).

This combining of drugs, coupled with smaller adolescent bodies (the average person of 175 pounds can oxidize or neutralize about one ounce of alcohol per hour), and little drug tolerance, can for the adolescent contribute to reducing the time from misuse to dependence to as little as two years. Now we can begin to understand a diagnosis of chemical dependence at age 13, 14 or 15 years of age. A high percentage of today's adolescents began to experiment with drugs in the sixth grade and are abusing them by the time they enter high school.

The "Adolescent Substance Abuse Fact Sheet" reveals some facts and figures about the magnitude of the problem.

In the Spring 1987 issue of *Alcoholism Update* published by the Milwaukee County Council on Alcoholism, an article entitled, "Did You Know," states: "Alcohol is America's No. 1 drug problem among youth." In 1985, an estimated 4.6 million adolescents aged 14 to 17 experienced negative consequences of alcohol use, e.g. arrest, involvement in an accident, or impairment of health or school performance.

Nearly 100,000 10-and 11-year-olds reported getting drunk at least once a week in 1985.

About one-third of the fourth graders (9-year-olds) said children their age pressured others to drink beer, wine and liquor; the figure increased to nearly 80 percent in high school. Nearly a third of high school seniors have said that most or all of their friends get drunk at least once a week.

Forty percent of the seniors have participated in the "party drinking syndrome," that is, consumed five or more drinks on one occasion, at least once in the preceding two weeks. Thirty percent did so on two or more occasions, and 20 percent did so three or more times in the designated two weeks. Only a third of the seniors thought there was a risk in this type of binge drinking.

Drinking differences between boys and girls are diminishing. The number of female drinkers has been increasing more rapidly than the number of young male drinkers.

In my 30 years as a chaplain in chemical dependence treatment centers, I have observed the popularity of specific drugs change. In my early years, alcohol was king, almost exclusively so. Though it is still king, it has experienced stiff competition the past 15 to 20 years from marijuana (pot) and most recently from cocaine, the most destructive drug today in my opinion. (During my seven years as the staff chaplain for the adolescent unit at De Paul Rehabilitation Hospital in Milwaukee, the adolescents on our unit ranged in age from 13 to 17, male and female.)

In the July–August 1986 issue of a newsletter entitled, *Staying Well*, published by the Foundation for Chiropractic Education and Research, Des Moines, Iowa, cocaine, marijuana, and alcohol are referred to as the "Deadly Trio." Four quotations from that newsletter are striking: "While Americans are actually consuming 4 percent less hard liquor than they were in 1980, the number of booze addicts has increased 8 percent to 12 million—including 3 million teenagers."

"Twenty years ago, fewer than 2 million people had tried smoking 'pot' or 'grass.' Now the National Institute on Drug Abuse estimates there are over 10 times that many regular users—17.4 million adults and 2.7 million children and adolescents. Of the 1.2 million who will smoke marijuana for the first time this year, nearly a million will be 17 or younger. In fact, some children in fourth and fifth grades smoke it regularly."

"Despite its relatively high price ($100 to $125 a gram) cocaine has approximately 25 million regular users and an estimated 5 million 'coke junkies'—serious addicts."

"Alcoholism and drug abuse are progressive, disabling diseases that involve the compulsive, repetitive use of mood-and mind-altering substances. These illnesses can impair health, damage family and social relationships, jeopardize careers, and cause legal problems."

However—There Is Treatment!

For too long a time, the popular phrase accepted as gospel was, "You can't help the alcoholic until he or she wants help." Or, "They have to hit their bottom," which for many was synonymous with Skid Row. As a result of that philosophy many addicts died alone—in box cars, in the alleys, on the waterfronts, burned to death or suicides. Today we have a much more human, caring, life-saving phrase, "Let's help them to want help," or "Let's raise the bottom."

By a process known as *intervention* dependents are helped to seek help and brought to the reality of their illness. It is a form of "tough love." You need to love your children enough to let them hurt. The pain has to exceed the pleasure. As long as your children have enablers or rescuers, people who relieve them from the responsibility for their inappropriate behavior, there is really no need for them to change, to give up the drugs. Intervention calls for withdrawing all support systems. The chemically dependent must be helped to experience the full, total, complete consequences of all behavior related to the drugs.

Intervention is necessary, only after you are convinced your child has a drug problem but refuses to recognize it and is in a stage of denial where all forms of treatment are rejected.

Intervention begins when you, as a parent, have worked through your own denial and have sought professional help at a treatment center or perhaps a council on alcoholism. You need to be assured, first of all, that you are not the cause of your child's chemical dependence and that you are doing the most loving thing you can by initiating the intervention.

The intervention counselor will ask you, the parent, to solicit the assistance of as many people as possible for the intervention—brothers or sisters, grandparents, neighbors, friends, an employer, the pastor, perhaps a physician or guidance counselor from high school. Solicit the help of anyone who might have a personal awareness of your child's drug abuse. You want people who are genuinely concerned, who will be willing to present material evidence, in a loving, not accusatory or judgmental manner.

The barrier of denial must be broken down by having each member of the intervention team write out a list of specific instances or experiences where the dependent person's abuse of the drugs has hurt, embarrassed, or offended the team member. You must be specific, listing date and place wherever possible. I call this the "symptom list." The dependent person might deny the symptom if only one person lists it; but if six, eight, or more people, all friends of the dependent, present a symptom list, denial is much more difficult.

After the counselor has again explained chemical dependence to the team, has again emphasized the need to break down the barrier of denial, and has stressed the importance of the symptom list, he will ask for team commitment to follow through to the end. Any member of the intervention team who has doubts about being willing or able to follow through should be excused. One weak link in the intervention can be very defeating. The dependent person will again latch on to that rescuer.

On the agreed-upon date and place of the intervention, the entire team walks in on the dependent person, as a surprise. The counselor facilitates the process, explaining to the person that all are there because they are concerned about the dependent's drug abuse, that all love the person very much and all have something to say about the effect that abuse has had upon the dependent. The dependent person is kindly asked to refrain from making any comments until all have read their symptom list.

Each intervention team member begins by assuring the dependent person of his love and concern, reads the symptom list, and concludes by encouraging the dependent person to seek treatment, assuring the person of ongoing support during and after treatment. After all have read their symptom list, the counselor asks what the person is willing to do in the face of all the evidence of chemical dependence.

Remember the goal of intervention is treatment. The intervention team must now be prepared to lovingly counter any denial, argument, or rationalization against treatment. The team must stick to its previous commitment and not accept anything short of treatment. You, the parents, must at this time be willing to state the ultimatum very firmly, yet lovingly, that unless your child agrees to treatment, he/she will have to leave home. But you must also speak very convincingly of your support and involvement while your child is in treatment as well as when returning home after treatment. This requires "tough love."

Perhaps you have some doubt as to the effectiveness of someone entering treatment against his will. Statistics indicate that the recovery rate is just as successful among those who enter treatment under duress as it is among those who enter voluntarily.

Two significant things happen, whether they enter under duress or voluntarily; first of all they are detoxed, so after a day or two, being free from the effect of the drugs, they can begin to think clearly, make rational judgments, and remember. Secondly, as they live with other dependent patients, they begin to realize that they are not alone, they begin to identify with them, and they begin to recognize attitudes and behavior in themselves that they were told about in their intervention.

In the treatment process they gain insight about themselves, their relationship to other people and their own self-image, all of which helps them to see how the drugs have distorted relationships and deadened feelings. They begin to sense how much more satisfying a natural high can be.

Dealing with Guilt

Under the influence of the drugs, your son or daughter did things that normally would not have been done. Under the influence of the drugs they become capable of doing things which are totally contrary to their sense of values. They lie, they shoplift, they steal money or other items from the home that can be pawned, they take your car without permission, they become very argumentative, verbally or perhaps even physically abusive, they are arrested, they become involved sexually, engaged in prostitution or selling their bodies for drugs—especially if they become involved in cocaine—or have an abortion.

A host of other wrongs or sins may have been committed—all of which can be condoned by them so long as they are under the influence of the drugs. But once in treatment, once detoxed, once the effect of the chemicals is no longer there and they are faced with the personal responsibility for their past life, then the pain, the remorse, the shame, and the guilt weigh heavily upon them.

The reality of their past passes condemningly before them as they work through the fourth step of the AA program, which says, "I made a searching and fearless, moral inventory of myself." Then, after having written out their inventory, they are ready for their fifth step, to confess, "I admitted to God, to myself, and to another human being the exact nature of my wrongs."

Here at De Paul we refer to this as "dumping the garbage." The fifth step is absolutely confidential. It is a statement of confession shared only with God and another human being. In most cases, here at De Paul, I am that other "human being." Even though very few of the adolescent patients here at De Paul have a personal relationship with God, for the most part they are very receptive to hearing about a God who is loving, forgiving, and accepting.

I frequently have the girls who are experiencing guilt due to sexual involvement read the story of the woman taken in adultery in John 8, with an emphasis on the last three short but direct statements of the Lord: "I do not condemn you either; go, but do not sin again." I tell them, "If you want release from the guilt, and if you want the peace of forgiveness, then you must be willing to make a total commitment for change—do not sin again."

But is forgiveness total and complete? That is the incredulous comment from those who say "I stole $7,000 from my dad's vault——I smashed my mom's car—I ran away and lived on the road with a trucker—I worked for a pimp—I had an abortion." Many of the adolescents I see think of forgiveness in terms of human limitations. Little white lies can be forgiven, or stealing small amounts of money, or staying away from home a night or two—well anyone should be willing to overlook, forgive, that. But "what I've done," it seems to them is unpardonable and too awful to ever be forgiven. But again, there is that clear word of Scripture. 1 John, 1:7 tells us, "The blood of Jesus Christ, God's Son, cleanses me from ALL sin." The Prophet Isaiah assures us of this same truth in chapter 1 verse 18, "The Lord says, 'Now let's settle the matter. You are stained red with sin, but I will wash you as clean as snow. Although your stains are deep red, you will be white as wool.' "

There is yet one other barrier to forgiveness. I suspect it is the result of an old, often heard remark, "I can forgive—but I'll never forget." So, the adolescent too, is concerned about forgetting their sins, but especially also, "Will Dad or Mom ever forget what I've done?" Again, they see this from the human element. God speaks of forgiving and forgetting in the same breath. It's as though God knew we might have difficulty with the forgetting part, so He tells us on three occasions that the two go together. The three references are in Jeremiah 31:34; Hebrews 8:12, and Hebrews 10:17. The wording is almost identical, "I will forgive their iniquity, and I will remember their sins no more." You may not forget the incident, but that incident, once forgiven, should never be brought back in condemnation again.

For many, the fifth step is a very painful accounting of "the exact nature of my wrong." But as they sit quietly, reviewing in their mind what we have talked about in regard to their total commitment for change, God's full forgiveness and forgetting—the relief begins to show. The weight is gone. The smile returns. There is a sense of self-worth that enables them to leave treatment, confident of their sobriety. And it could happen only, because you as a parent could "love them enough to let them hurt," and in that intervention gave them a realistic ultimatum, treatment or loose all support.

Be Supportive

Here at De Paul we plan for a predischarge family conference. It is very important for all members in the family to have a clear understanding of expectations. What are the rules? Are all members of the family agreed upon the rules and expectations? Will there be room for compromise? How are exceptions going to be handled and if someone feels the need for a change, how will that be handled?

I feel a working through of the first part of the ninth step by the dependent person and the parents is vitally important. That step says, "I became willing to make direct amends, wherever possible." It's a mutual clearing of the air. It's an excellent time for a mutual sharing of love and forgiveness. It's a good time for the parents to make a statement in regard to "forgive and forget." It's a time for a renewed parent—child relationship.

Since an ongoing support system, such as an aftercare program, AA (Alcoholics Anonymous), NA (Narcotics Anonymous), or CA (Cocaine Anonymous), is so vitally important in maintaining a drug free life-style, parents must be willing to arrange transportation for the child to attend these meetings on a weekly basis.

Nurture your children. Love them. Set limits for them. Lovingly discipline them. Be a positive role model. Be available to them. Pray for them and with them. And may you all, "turn your life and your will over to the care of God."

LEVELS OF ALCOHOL USE

I. Experimental Use - Early Junior High
(Often unplanned-sneak drinks, etc.—little use of "harder drugs")
1. Occasional beer drinking—glue sniffing—weekends with friends.
2. Easy to get high—(low tolerance).
3. Thrill of acting grown up—defying parents.

II. More Regular Use - Late Junior High
(More money involved—parents become aware—"grounding"—drug using friends not introduced to parents—lying—school activities dropped—grades drop—truancy increases—non-drug using friends dropped)
4. Tolerance increases with increased use—"Everyone does it"—staying out late—all night.
5. Beer mostly—willing to suffer hangover.
6. Proud to be able to "handle it".
7. School skipping and weeknight using begins.
8. Blackouts.
9. Solitary use—fooling parents, etc.
10. Preoccupation with use begins—source of supply becomes a worry.
11. Use during day—experiment with barbs, speed, acid, dust.

III. Daily Preoccupation
(Possible "dealing" or "fronting"—possible court problems—probation—may try to quit—straight friends dropped—owe money—more truancy and fights with parents)
12. Use of harder drugs increases.
13. Money for drugs increases.
14. No longer just "high" but "loaded".
15. All activities include booze and drugs.
16. Theft for money.
17. Solitary use increase—isolation.
18. Lying and hiding drugs.

IV. Dependency
(Guilt feelings increased—low self-image and self-hate—continued denial of problem—school dropped—dealing increases—paranoia—money for drugs increase—total loss of control over use)
19. Getting high during school and/or work—can't face the day without drugs.
20. Possible use of injectable drugs—friends are burnouts.
21. Normal—"stoned".
22. Loss of weight—memory suffers—flashbacks—thoughts of suicide.

ADOLESCENT SUBSTANCE ABUSE FACT SHEET*

Fact 1
There is a wide range of usage by the senior year in high school.
93% have at least tried alcohol.
74% have at least tried cigarettes.
60% have at least tried marijuana.

Fact 2
Substance abuse is a part of the adolescent experience. We are not simply dealing with a phenomenon of exposure; substance abuse is viewed as normal behavior by the adolescent population.
83% of high school seniors saw some friends drunk during the course of the week.
35% of the same group saw most or all of their friends intoxicated on a weekly basis.

Fact 3
Adolescent substance abuse is not just a "social" phenomenon. Adolescents are using to become intoxicated.
65-70% reported getting very high or moderately high when they use.
65-70% reported the high lasting 3-5 hours.

Fact 4
Young people are experimenting with drugs and alcohol increasingly at a younger age.
Class of 1979—first use grade 6-8.
Class of 1975—first use grade 8-10.

Fact 5
Chemically dependent adolescents are the children of chemically dependent parents.
40-60% of chemically dependent children have one or two chemically dependent parents.
We are seeing more drugs in more young people at a younger age with greater intensity for a longer period of time. This has enormous implications in terms of normal physical development and normal, healthy psychosocial development. The phenomenon is not one of less usage but of a wider acceptance.

*Data from longitudinal study of 3,000 high school seniors. Presented by Dr. Robert Pandina, Rutgers University.

The Disease of Chemical Dependency in Adolescence

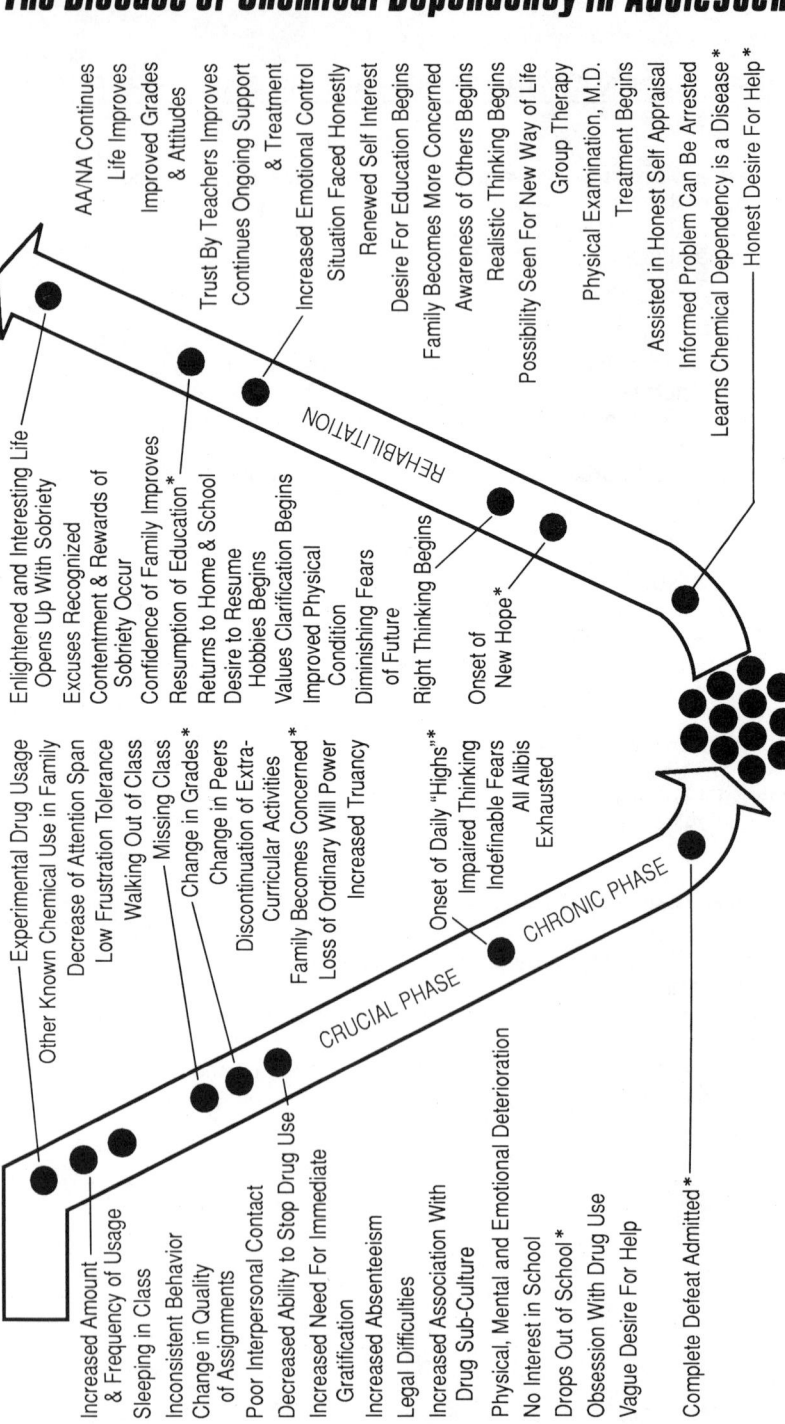

Crucial Phase (descending)

- Experimental Drug Usage
- Other Known Chemical Use in Family
- Decrease of Attention Span
- Low Frustration Tolerance
- Walking Out of Class
- Missing Class
- Change in Grades*
- Change in Peers
- Discontinuation of Extra-Curricular Activities
- Family Becomes Concerned*
- Loss of Ordinary Will Power
- Increased Truancy

- Increased Amount & Frequency of Usage
- Sleeping in Class
- Inconsistent Behavior
- Change in Quality of Assignments
- Poor Interpersonal Contact
- Decreased Ability to Stop Drug Use
- Increased Need For Immediate Gratification
- Increased Absenteeism
- Legal Difficulties

Chronic Phase

- Onset of Daily "Highs"*
- Impaired Thinking
- Indefinable Fears
- All Alibis Exhausted

- Increased Association With Drug Sub-Culture
- Physical, Mental and Emotional Deterioration
- No Interest in School
- Drops Out of School*
- Obsession With Drug Use
- Vague Desire For Help
- Complete Defeat Admitted*

COMPULSIVE DRUG USE CONTINUES IN VICIOUS CYCLES

Rehabilitation (ascending)

- Onset of New Hope*
- Right Thinking Begins
- Diminishing Fears of Future
- Improved Physical Condition
- Values Clarification Begins
- Desire to Resume Hobbies Begins
- Returns to Home & School
- Resumption of Education*
- Confidence of Family Improves
- Contentment & Rewards of Sobriety Occur
- Excuses Recognized
- Enlightened and Interesting Life Opens Up With Sobriety

- Honest Desire For Help*
- Learns Chemical Dependency is a Disease*
- Informed Problem Can Be Arrested
- Assisted In Honest Self Appraisal
- Treatment Begins
- Physical Examination, M.D.
- Group Therapy
- Possibility Seen For New Way of Life
- Realistic Thinking Begins
- Awareness of Others Begins
- Family Becomes More Concerned
- Desire For Education Begins
- Renewed Self Interest
- Situation Faced Honestly
- Increased Emotional Control
- Continues Ongoing Support & Treatment
- Trust By Teachers Improves
- Improved Grades & Attitudes
- Life Improves
- AA/NA Continues

Points to Remember

1. There are clear behavioral changes which can alert you to possible drug abuse and/or drug dependence.
2. Most abusers today abuse more than one drug.
3. Drug dependence time is greatly reduced in adolescents, so that it is possible for a 13-or-14-year old to be dependent.
4. Through the intervention process, it is possible to get drug dependent people to seek help and see the reality of their illness without "hitting bottom."
5. Parents contemplating intervention need first to work through their own denial of the problem.
6. The goal of intervention is treatment. Success rates are as high for people who enter treatment under duress as for those who enter voluntarily.
7. Recognize the part guilt plays for those involved in abuse and proclaim clear words of forgiveness.
8. People in recovery need support after going through a program. Stay with them! Pray with them!

Violence and Victims: Making Nobody's Day

Betty Brusius

*T*he local newspaper and TV headlines were full of the news. Eighteen-year-old Tom was arrested for raping a woman. How could that be? Little Tommy—so kind and helpful as a small child. Someone remembered how upset he had been when a playmate deliberately stepped on a toad.

According to psychologist Neil Malamuth, between 35 percent and 60 percent of male college students at UCLA, Stanford University, and the University of Manitoba in Canada reported that there is at least some likelihood they would rape a woman or use force to get sex, if they were certain of getting away with it. Whose sons are they? Surely not yours! And surely not mine! Whose daughters will be the victims? Hopefully not yours, and hopefully not mine! And yet . . . these sons and daughters will be somebody's!

Susan, a classmate of Tom's, was about the only person not surprised when she heard the news. She had dated Tom a few times. Now she sat and reflected on those dates she'd had with him. She had seen him in the halls and was especially attracted to him because he was a young man of few words, the strong, silent type. He didn't date much and this was a challenge to her.

Susan hadn't dated too much either and didn't know quite how to get him interested in her. She had looked through her supply of magazines and tried a new hairstyle. She read a few articles on "how to get your man." She saw an ad for a brand of perfume she hadn't tried. It was guaranteed to make men wild.

Armed with advice from her magazines, she initiated a conversation with Tom in the school hall on Monday. Sure enough, he sat with her at lunch that day, and by Friday night they had a date.

Susan was different from some of her girlfriends because she knew where she was headed in life. She was going to college and "saving" herself sexually until she married. She thought the girls that messed around were foolish.

Tom, unfortunately, did not have the benefit of a good Christian training leading to a wholesome attitude (as discussed in Chapter 1) that sex is a gift of God, that a redeemed person knows all gifts are to be used responsibly and that in this case his desire for physical gratification was really selfish and ought to be deferred.

On their second date Susan was thrilled when Tom kissed her good night. It meant he was beginning to care about her. On their third date he kept his arm around her during the whole movie. The night of the fourth date they had gone to a dance and were getting into the car to go to Susan's house. Then the nightmare began for Susan. Tom drove his car to a secluded road, pulled over to the curb, turned off the engine for what Susan assumed would be a little hugging and kissing. And then . . . Susan's plans and dreams seemed to end. Tom forced himself on her sexually. As he began, Susan protested the first advances, but to no avail. She realized quickly she could not fight him off. Before she knew it, it was all over . . . and she thought her life was, too. She felt used, dirty. She blamed herself for what had happened and didn't believe that she could ever trust a male again.

Everyone was in bed at her house when she got home. So she was able to go to her room quietly. She didn't sleep that night, or very well for many nights after. Who could she tell? Who would believe her? Why should anyone believe her when she'd worked so hard to get Tom interested in her. Everyone would say it served her right, or . . . what did she expect? She was alone with her shame and humiliation.

Susan had experienced what we now call "date rape" or "acquaintance rape"—loosely interpreted to be unwanted sexual intercourse with someone you have willingly gone with, as opposed to rape by a stranger.

Date rape is only one of the frequent expressions of violence in North American society, one of the most advanced and at the same time most violent societies ever to exist. There are certainly many causes for these ills in our society, but the overt and covert messages aimed at children which promote and glorify suicide, rape, and sado-masochism, have to be numbered among the contributing factors.

Some types of violence are performed in public and yet considered entertainment. The sport of boxing regularly draws attention for its violent nature. Groups from the U.S. and Canada picketed boxing competition at the Pan-American Games in Indianapolis, Indiana, asking that the sport be dropped from future Pan-Am Games. They cited several dozen research studies showing brain damage to boxers, and another 20 studies showing that boxing increases tendencies towards anger and aggression in spectators.

Professional wrestling is another major form of sports entertainment which is promoted by television media. It causes much discussion, whenever it reappears on network schedules, as to whether it is a show or a sport. Researcher Gordon W. Russell has presented two scientific studies showing that the viewing of professional wrestling has harmful effects on normal adult and adolescent viewers.

Those who doubt the power of wrestling matches to produce violent behavior among spectators need only attend one such match in person and observe the crowd behavior in the stands and in the hallways.

Tommy had never been to either a boxing or wrestling match, but his father was a great fan. One thing Tommy had noticed was that when his dad's favorite opponent lost a match, he was really grouchy for a few hours, so Tommy stayed away from him.

Tommy couldn't understand why his dad wouldn't let him watch with the other men, since he was always stressing being a man. He quit the baseball team when his dad told him that he wasn't tough enough to be on the team.

His father was not an uncaring father. In fact, he loved his family very much according to his own understanding. He was good at his job—put everything he had into it because he believed his main role in the family was to provide a good material living for them. He was able to be "in charge" of his life, his surroundings, at all times. He could take care of his own. He was a "man's man"—and his son would be one, too, if he had anything to say about it. He had some hunting buddies, some "girlie" magazines, and a supply of off-color jokes to trade with his buddies. He scoffed at his friends who sat in church every Sunday morning. He didn't need God. He was doing just fine, thank you!

Meanwhile, Tommy did spend a lot of time in his room watching TV. Every day when he got home from school he would have a snack and then watch cartoons and other shows until dinner, then back to the TV for several more hours.

As a young child, his favorite heroes were Superman types. He loved taking a towel and putting it over his shoulders and jumping off of his dresser, emulating in his limited way Superman feats. His mom thought this was cute and was able to find Superman sheets and pillowcases for his room.

Thousands of little boys in our culture go through the stages of watching the superhero characters, playing cops and robbers, getting into the video games, and later on experience the magazines and movies which emphasize pornography, illicit sex, violence, and degradation of all human beings. Teenagers are actually major consumers of so-called adult magazines.

All of us are surrounded by ideas that are unhealthy—physically, emotionally, spiritually—and yet we often take them so lightly, thinking they are doing us little harm. If a member of a religious cult such as Hare Krishna came to our front door and asked if he or she could spend four hours a night with our teen, we would be horrified. Yet, the truth is that many of our teens are catching attitudes and ideas far more destructive and contrary to our values through avenues such as TV which we see daily and take for granted as part of our everyday lives.

Even a family with *National Geographic* as their only magazine subscription can receive an envelope marked "Sexually-oriented Ad." A recent mailing offered 12 hardcore video bestsellers, all in full color, all for only $4.16 each. A picture and description for each of the 12 is included. *China De Sade* is described as "a hilarious spoof of bondage films with the actors having a lot of fun playing around with torture, bondage, and rapelike sex rather than being serious about it." Another video, *Nicole, the Story of O,* is described as "elegantly photographed and setting the cinematic standards for sophisticated S&M [sado-masochism]."

A direct-mail advertisement from *Playboy* says, "Ever since Hugh Hefner published a photograph of Marilyn Monroe in 1953, *Playboy* has kept its finger on the pulse of America's intelligent, sophisticated men—and made it beat faster. I'm sure I don't have to tell you about the attractive women that *Playboy* can bring into your home each month, women who will make you growl, chew on your shoelaces, and fan yourself with a celery stalk . . . Let me show you why 12,000,000 men chew on their shoelaces anticipating their next monthly issue of *Playboy.*"

Research indicates that teenage males are frequent readers of "girlie" magazines and other sexually oriented materials readily available in the average community. Law enforcement officials report that pedophiles use such materials along with regular sexually oriented ads to entice children into sexual acts and to duplicate specific scenes and poses.

One argument for allowing the continued availability and distribution of material which is so obviously harmful and of so little redeeming social value has been that it has no effect on normal individuals. However, young people such as Tom appear normal and yet are obviously disturbed enough to commit the acts which they do. Some of the other factors which contribute to this "normal" young man committing anti-social acts are:

- no religious life inside/outside of the home
- encouragement or at least permissiveness in idolizing superhero characters
- unmonitored and undiscussed use of TV
- no one with whom to spend time sorting out the images presented to him by peers and media
- poor modeling by his father through his emphasis on "control" and devaluation of women, on "things," on "being quiet," and an unhealthy "macho" image

- a passive mother, a victim of that "macho" image, who has sunk to a "survival" mode so as not to "stir things up"
- pornographic literature
- violent/sexually oriented rock music
- peer attitudes

All of us can identify with many of the above. Parents are constantly being called upon to deal with factors that tear away at the values they wish to pass on to children and often underestimate the effects of the pulls and tugs of society.

Whether we are trying to break patterns in our households that have been passed from generation to generation or fighting new negative influences, we need to look at the factors which are shaping our lives and the lives of our children and seek out resources to help us talk to our teens—first about general issues, and then about the violence in our lives and theirs.

We can help them to see what values they are forming, some seemingly by osmosis, that are contrary to what we are trying to do as Christian parents striving to live worthy of who we are in Jesus Christ—as we do our best to live our faith, as we are active in Christian education programs, regular church attendance, and regular family devotions.

Because I had a daughter that was into rock music, I needed to become familiar with it myself. I listened to it, although the beat often made me nervous. The argument that we had about music in our day–that what was happening was simply a phase that each age goes through–gave me little comfort. This was far more than entertainment or relaxation.

According to the *Parent's Music Resource Center 1985 Report*, rock music appears to have five major themes to which it turns again and again: They are hostile violent rebellion, substance abuse, sexual irresponsibility and perversion, violence, and the occult. Here are a few examples from the report:

Violent rebellion: While rock music has always stressed a desire for independence, today's youth are being encouraged to express their anger and independence in destructive ways. The heavy-metal band, Twisted Sister, released an album called *Stay Hungry,* which contains the hit song, "We're Not Going to Take It." The song was released as a video that portrayed a father being physically abused by the band. To be a member of the Twisted Sister fan club means that you don't let your parents tell you what to do.

Gene Simmons of Kiss in an interview with *Faces* magazine advised his young teen audience to ignore anybody who tries to tell them what to do—including parents—and instead go after their dreams.

The band, BlackLace, in its album *Unlaced* has a song, "Born to Raise Hell," warning that they are lean and mean and ready to take you down, and they are ready to see you dead rather than have you take what belongs to them. "You take what's mine. I was born to raise hell!" "Shout at the Devil" by the heavy-metal band Motley Crue says that the devil is anybody who tries to tell you what to do. It may be anybody—boss, teacher, or parents. They believe in getting rid of all authority figures if their music is to be taken seriously.

Violence in Rock Music

Many songs glorify suicide, revenge, sexual violence, and violence just for violence's sake. AC/DC's album, *Flat on the Wall*, includes graphic sex and alcohol abuse. The song, "Back in Business," which was also released as a single, calls for just one more drink before killing a partner who is to remain passive while the degradation takes place. At least one young man took the advice of AC/DC and killed himself with his father's hunting rifle. He died beneath his AC/DC poster. In the background AC/DC was singing "Shoot to Thrill."

It's no secret that today's teenagers live in a world more insecure than ever; pressure on young people is at an all-time high. For many, depression and alienation lead to thoughts of ending it all. Sadly enough, many hear rock musicians presenting suicide as the best alternative. Ronnie James Deal's album, *Sacred Heart*, includes the song "Shoot-shoot" which intones the feelings of desperation when your back is to the wall. If somebody points a gun at you, you say, "Go ahead and shoot," because there are no options left. The last sound is the pulling of a trigger and a blast.

These are only brief excerpts from two of the five previously mentioned areas of concern. It would be helpful to obtain a complete copy of this report from the Parent's Music Resource Center, 655 15th St., N.W., Suite 300, Washington, D.C., 20005.

Why Knock Rock? available through your public library, is helpful on the topic of rock and violence. Browsing through the rock magazines at newsstands is another source. You will discover that there are more groups than you have ever imagined. Some of the group names and the titles of albums and songs are enough to tell that the content is violent.

The April 1987 issue of *Metal Mania* magazine contained information on the following groups and albums:

Anvil Bitch released their first album, *Rise to Offend*, with the songs "Neckbreaker," "Apostle to Hell," "Time to Die," and "To the Grave."

An album by Sacrifice was scheduled to include "After Life," "Cyanide," "Forever Enslaved," "Pyro-Kinesis," and "Terror Strike."

Artillery released the album *Terror Squad*.

Aggression released their first album through Face Melt Records in the U.S. The line-up consists of guitarists Burn and Death, Butchers on vocals, Dug on bass, and Gate on drums.

Slaughter released their debut album, *Strappado*. It included the songs "Maim to Please," "Parasite," "—— Of Death," "Tortured Soul," and "Nocturnal Hell."

Satan's Host released its second album, *Midnight Wind*. The band consists of guitarist Satan Patrick Evil, bass-thumper Belial, D. Lucifer Steele on drums, and vocalist Leviathan Thisiren who played under the name of The Tyrant while he was in Jag Panzer. Songs on the album are "Witches Return," "Faces of Fire," and "Black Sunday."

Two more quotes show that some of the most frightening exponents of violence not only are conscious of their effect on the minds of innocent young people, they freely express their intentions:

"Atmospheres are going to come through music, because music is a spiritual thing of its own. You can hypnotize people with music, and when you get people at the weakest point, you can preach to them into the subconscious what we want to say." Jimi Hendrix, *Why Knock Rock?* p. 76.

"I figured that the only thing to do was steal their kids. I still think it's the only thing to do. By saying that, I'm not talking about kidnapping. I'm just talking about changing young people's value systems which removes them from their parent's world very effectively." David Crosby of Crosby, Stills, Nash, and Young. *Why Knock Rock?* p. 96.

Our family met one of those young people who had been removed effectively from the mainstream of society into a world of violence that was created within his own mind and lived out in the lives of those who loved and cared for him. He was one of the countless thousands of young people who seem lost in a world which they don't understand.

One of our teenage daughters befriended Kevin even though his life was so completely different from hers. Kevin had been abused all of his life and dropping out of school, had retreated into glue-sniffing and alcohol abuse. Unemployed, he didn't even show up in the statistics because he was no longer looking for a job. He was the kind of young person featured in a cable television production on teenage drug abusers, "Stoned in America." Teenager after teenager talked about staying high just to be able to get through one day at a time.

Our daughter thought she could be a positive influence on Kevin and help him turn his life around. He appeared quiet, shy, withdrawn, and even polite. Believing that everybody has potential, she got a high school equivalency book so she could help him study for the test, made calls to find out how and where he should apply for a job, and even got him to church one Sunday. What she was soon to find out was that when they talked on the phone about all the good, possible goals for him, he was enthusiastic. But in reality he was not capable of carrying through any of the plans, and they remained fruitless, frustrating dreams which only caused him to feel more worthless. Kevin's motivational level, already low as a result of the models which he had experienced, was diminished more by his habitual glue-sniffing and beer drinking so that he simply couldn't do anything.

When our daughter tried to break off their friendship, our nightmare began. It lasted for about a year—a long year of telephone calls in the middle of the night—only to be hung up on. We all became the targets of the foulest of language and threats. I lived with fear day and night for her safety and ours.

Kevin's behavior became more and more violent. We found out that he was frequently involved in fights and while under the influence of drugs had to be subdued by his brother. During at least one of these episodes he stabbed his brother. Of course, Kevin felt remorseful after each episode.

He had been committed to a correctional institution several times, obtained work in construction, and found a girlfriend who cared for him even though he beat her regularly. Finally, after one such beating, he felt remorseful, overdosed, and died. As he was dying, he was asked, "Kevin, do you want to live?" He nodded, "yes," before he died.

Many teens today know other teens like Kevin—victims of a violent society who in turn become victimizers themselves. We cannot protect them from the violence or those who commit it.

But we can talk with our teens to help them:

- feel better about themselves,
- monitor their own behavior,
- learn to be more perceptive about friends and acquaintances,
- see that the media has a powerful influence on our thinking,
- choose their dating partners more carefully.

You may be able to add some more of your ideas to these suggestions.

Talk, talk, talk. Sounds easy, right? All you do is say, "Tom, let's talk about life," as you pat the seat next to you on the couch. *Wrong*! Chances are with an approach like that, you are both in trouble.

Most teens really *do* want to be able to talk to parents, but I know from personal experience it was difficult for me to listen to some things because I felt I had to moralize. It would have been much easier for me to listen to someone else's teen saying the same things—a teen I didn't feel responsible for raising in difficult times. One of my teenage daughters complained that many of our conversations turned into my "lectures." She was right, because I felt that if I were silent, that would be giving consent to a value that I didn't hold.

I know I bungled many attempts, but I still believe that trying something is better than throwing up our hands and declaring parent-teen communication efforts as useless. That same daughter sent me a letter after her marriage letting me know that those many late nights I sat up talking with her during her teen years were not wasted, that even though it sometimes appeared she wasn't listening, she really was.

Yet, knowing more about communication today, I would do some things differently:

a. I would gather enough information on a topic to feel confident of my position, enough not to feel I had to defend the position. The teen already feels insecure enough and needs me to be secure in my position.

b. Another of my struggles has been to want to solve things for my teens. What I needed was patience and respectful listening in troubling situations. My daughters then would have been able to talk out the options with me. When I "solved" their problem, I shut them off from the valuable opportunity of being responsible for their own actions. In retrospect I can see that I was trying to *control* because of mistakenly thinking that my responsibility as a parent meant that it would be possible to shelter my children from the realities of life.

c. Well, if the "couch" doesn't work, what kind of setting will? Two places worked best for me. The first one is the car, surprisingly enough. Maybe it's because it doesn't seem like a planned talk, or contrived setting. It might be because you are busy driving and the teen can look out the window or down at the floor, and is not forced into eye contact. Whatever the reasons, it seems to work well for parents and teens alike.

How do you start? Turn off the radio—share something in your day that involves a struggle for you, and some feelings. This will loosen up both of you; the teen can see that you don't have all the answers. Or, say something nice about a friend of the teen's of whom you approve, and before you know it, you're off!

I found another good place to talk with young teens is their bedroom after their light was off. This will probably only work well with younger teens, but it's worth a try with yours. I found that if I sat on the bed in the dark and initiated a conversation in a laid-back way, the early teen shared a lot of the concerns that would not have come out in other ways.

d. Do not expect miracles in your discussions, but do persist in your statements of what you believe about life issues and why. Our teens really need to know our values.

It is important to share *your own* faith life. I think it is a mistake to assume we are automatically communicating what we believe and practice as God-fearing adults, or that our teens understand us.

One of our daughters at the age of 14 refused to pray with us at the dinner table one night. When asked why, she said she didn't feel like she was really talking to God because we used the same prayers every night. After some discussion we had to admit she had a point. We dropped rote prayers and began spontaneous ones that ultimately included the teens' concerns for classmates, teachers, and their own joys and struggles. About the same time I started to keep a piece of paper on the kitchen table to which every day I added new people and things about which to pray. I told the girls they were welcome to add anything to the list. For some time the list showed only my handwriting, and then I almost jumped for joy one morning when I saw a daughter's handwriting added to the list. That was the beginning of spiritual communication opening up that continues to this day.

Establishing meaningful communication gives us the opportunity to discuss more serious issues—self-esteem, the value of other humans, the seriousness of *using* people, insensitivity to others, victimization, and violent influences around us.

- Read and discuss with your teens the magazines they are bringing home or which they talk about. Look at the articles, the pictures, the ads. What kinds of values do they portray? Are they consistent with your faith? Out of harmony? Talk about what it means to confess one thing and practice something else.

- Listen to the same music your teen is hearing. Check out the albums. Attend a rock concert to be able to see what happens. What does your teen like? The beat? The noise? What is the thinking and purpose of the group? Is there Christian rock available? Is it an acceptable alternative? For your teen? For you?

- Be persistent and consistent in expressing what you believe and why. Depend on the Holy Spirit to be effective when God's word is proclaimed.

- Pay attention to advertising in the various media. What is the current emphasis? How are people treated? As objects? What do they say about the worth of all people?
- Be aware of the popular television programs. Note the fluctuation from illicit sex to violence, depending upon how vocal the public is against these negatives and how much support producers and sponsors perceive. Note the place of alcohol and the references to drugs in various programs.
- Read the reviews of movies and actually attend one occasionally. Find out what young people are seeing. What movies are being aimed specifically at the teen market? How are violence and sex used? Does the audience identify with the perpetrators or the victims?
- If you have daughters and they read romantic novels, spend some time yourself reading them. What are the recurring themes? Virgins waiting to be forced into sex and loving it? What stereotypes are there about what it means to be a man? a woman? How the sexes treat each other?
- Video games are very popular and generally very violent. At any given time there are over 400 games available and 80–90 percent are violent. Go to a video gallery and play some of the games yourself. Note what effects they have on you before talking about them with your teens.
- Both spectator and participant sports can be very healthy outlets for people of any age. Unfortunately, many sports are spiced with violence. Boxing and wrestling were mentioned earlier, but other sports are also well-known for the violence associated with them. Hockey is known for fights on the ice and riots among the fans. Soccer can be the cleanest of sports but its fans the most violent as evidenced by the riots in Europe and other countries. Even certain baseball teams are known for the violence in the stands, and there are stadiums which ban or limit beer sales.
- Talk to your teens—both male and female—about dating behavior. Rather than stressing the dangers of AIDS, STD (sexually transmitted diseases), and pregnancy, talk about what it means to treat others decently as creations of God, all fallen but redeemed.

Talk about what it means to respect yourself. Insist that you meet any dating partners, and even ask questions about their families.

■ Do not be afraid to set time limits. Curfews may not be popular, but your teen will respect you for being concerned and for setting limits. Many a teen has gotten out of a bad situation by saying, "I can't because I've got to be in by eleven."

One of my daughters sent me a Mother's Day poem which said in part: "When I was a teenager, I had my ups and downs, but you were always there. You reinforced my values and beliefs; you set a curfew because you cared . . . "

■ Finally, the best defense against the violence of our society is a loving, gentle approach to life which you live and mirror to your teen. Burn into your heart and mind the words of St. Paul to the Philippians: "Rejoice in the Lord always, I will say it again: Rejoice! Let your gentleness be evident to all. The Lord is near. Do not be anxious about anything, but in everything, by prayer and petition, with thanksgiving, present your requests to God. And the peace of God, which transcends all understanding, will guard your hearts and your minds in Christ Jesus.

"Finally, brothers, whatever is true, whatever is noble, whatever is right, whatever is pure, whatever is lovely, whatever is admirable—if anything is excellent or praiseworthy—think about such things. Whatever you have learned or received or heard from me, or seen in me—put it into practice. And the God of peace will be with you" (Phil. 4:4–9).

Points to Remember

1. Normal youth and adults in our society are confronted daily with programs and materials which desensitize to the violence all around us.
2. Certain types of violence are taken for granted simply as entertainment, for example, boxing, wrestling, football, hockey.
3. Parents tolerate influences in the home through the various media which would horrify parents if presented by cult members.
4. Parents need to read the words of rock songs in order to grasp the often violent and sexually violent messages.
5. Talk to your teens about their experiences with peers. Many teens

know other teens who are potential "burnouts" and more susceptible to violent actions.
6. Carefully establish what is your best avenue and time for communicating with your teen.
7. Share your faith life with your teen. Trust the Holy Spirit as you seek to live as one who has been redeemed by Jesus Christ!
8. The best defense against the violence of our society is a loving, gentle approach to life which you live and mirror to your teen.

"Turn That Thing Down!!!"

Annette Frank

"Turn that thing down!" These are familiar words in any household in which a teen or preteen lives, breathes, and listens to rock music. These words may be familiar not only because you've used them so often with your own young people, but perhaps because your parents said them when you were a teen also listening to rock music.

I've wondered, if we'd take the volume out of rock music, would it still be rock? Is it the loudness that makes it so great? Does having the volume on *loud* make the music sound better?

Sometimes I think teens turn their music to *loud*, not to annoy parents—but to build up a wall of sound around themselves—like a cocoon. Perhaps it is a need for privacy—a need to be alone for self-discovery, reflection, and exploration—that brings the desire to surround the self with a protective wall, a wall of self preservation, a wall of *sound*.

Stresses and demands dog our young people wherever they go. Parents, teachers, and peers, expecting certain conduct and accomplishments, are pulling our youth this way and that. Someone is always telling them what to do, where to be, and when to be there. As they struggle to find themselves and be themselves, perhaps the beat and sounds of rock music, and in some cases even the lyrics, provide a cushion from all their stressors. When the music is loud enough, the only thing that can be heard is the music. They don't hear the requests to help carry in the groceries or hang up their clothes or set the table or get their homework done. They aren't bothered by the demands of everyday life. The music is a barrier to those requests.

Perhaps the volume is what we initially find so disturbing about rock music, or any music. Loud sounds do nothing to soothe the overly stimulated nerves—nerves frazzled from a day at the workplace, driving through traffic, shopping at the grocery store, or just the everyday noises around us. Walking into our homes needing peace and calmness and being met by wall to wall, ceiling to floor resounding SOUND does nothing for our disposition. The first thing we do—or want to do—is shout "Turn that thing down!"

That reaction does nothing for any kind of positive relationships. The issue really isn't rock music; the issue is that we have a need for a few minutes of peace and quiet so that we can put off the stresses of the day. Now not only do we still have the frazzled nerves, but upset teens and upset relationships!

How do we deal with the loudness problem without causing more problems, more stresses? Do we ban rock music from the home? Do we banish the kids to their rooms, minus the stereo equipment, with the additional ban on any kind of noise, especially rock music? Saint Paul gives families some good advice in Ephesians "Children, obey your parents in the Lord, for this is right. 'Honor your father and mother'—which is the first command with a promise—'that it may go well with you and that you may enjoy long life on the earth.'

"Fathers, do not exasperate your children; instead, bring them up in the training and instruction of the Lord" (Eph. 6:1–4). If we take these words to heart, instead of yelling "Turn that thing down!" or banishing all tapes, videos, radios and the like to the trash can, we will work on a way to satisfy everyone's needs. A good place to start is with prayer. Pray for guidance and direction. Ask that the Lord show a solution where everyone's needs are met.

Maybe our teens are turning up the volume in an effort to understand the words to the music. If you've ever done this, you know the words are just as difficult to hear with the volume on loud. Perhaps it is just as well that the words are garbled. By not being able to understand what is being sung, we may be protecting our language sensitive ears. However, this is not facing the problem of the language being used.

Listen to the music of the early days of rock and roll, and it would seem almost tame and colorless put next to what we have today, and rock has not been around that long. Like other musical forms, it began simply. Unlike other musical forms, it developed rapidly—influencing or being influenced by today's society, technological advances, and electronic wizardry. We may well ask, "Do we influence rock (or TV or movies) or does rock influence us? Do we give shape to the values expressed in rock (TV, movies) or are these values shaping our values?" Looking at the roots of rock, we can see the origins of some of the themes, ideals, and values expressed in rock music. Some of them clash with our Christian perspective. Talking about them gives us starting points for family discussions, enabling us as parents to solidify our value systems and share with our teens our ideals, goals, and values for them—at the same time hearing their needs, goals, and values.

In the late 1940s, this music could be heard late at night on some of the AM radio stations in our cities. By the early 1950s, American youth had begun listening to these stations and hearing sounds that were foreign to the culture of middle class America, but sounds that nevertheless called out to the young person of the 1950s. What were they hearing? The crying sounds of the saxophone, the steady rhythm of drums, the desire for freedom, for opportunity, and for dreams to be fulfilled. These were the sounds and themes of a segment of America before *Brown vs. the Board of Education*, the peace marches, and Martin Luther King, Jr. These were the sounds of a people held down. These were sounds that parents often found alarming and threatening.

Television and rock grew up together and became important complements of one another. Early TV programs reviewing the "top ten" hits of the week included "Your Hit Parade" to be followed by "American Bandstand." "American Bandstand" gave young America an opportunity to hear the latest hits, watch the latest dances, and see the latest stars. In the 1980s the music video made its appearance bringing a whole new dimension to music—and a whole lot more concerns to parents.

Do we make a "big deal" out of rock when there may not be a reason? Does music influence us? In church worship, one of the components of the service is music. The purpose of the music is to reinforce the spoken word, support the emphasis of the service, and lead the congregation in worship. Music is present to influence the worshiper. Does it? Listen to the "beat" of the music during Christmas and Easter. It is often lively and upbeat. Some of it makes you want to tap your toes—even in church. Listen to the melodies and accompaniments. They are cheerful, celebrating, and exalting. Now switch to Lenten music. Often it is slower and mournful as it sets the tone for solemnity and repentance. Certainly one of the purposes of the music we hear in church is to influence us—and it does.

Let's look at another example. This may be used as a concrete case where music has had an influence on people, one that might be an example to use when talking with your teen. You might begin by saying, "I know you think I'm making a big deal out of the kind of music you're listening to, but I'm interested in what you like and what you do. I'm interested in the choices you make and the things that influence you. Yes, I know you've said you don't pay any attention to the words, you just listen to the instrumental sounds, but I'd like to talk with you about that.

"Do you remember a couple of years ago when people were concerned about the African nations that were suffering from drought conditions? Do you remember how many of the music celebrities took a personal interest in the starving and suffering people? Remember how they organized a way for ordinary people to support this cause and raise money to send to the hungry in Africa? Americans were urged to join 'Hands across America' one Sunday afternoon. At a specified time, hundreds of thousands of Americans joined hands along a given route that stretched from coast to coast and all these people held hands, singing 'We are the World.' It seemed that every time you listened to the radio or turned on the TV you heard 'We are the World.' Do you think music played any part in the reason those people were standing in that line?"

You might continue, "A giant, nationwide chorus singing its heart out is not easy to ignore. (If you were a part of that line, or drove or walked along it, you probably were moved by the experience.) How do you think the people participating in 'Hands across America' felt? They felt united, buoyant, proud, uplifted. Do you remember some of the pictures we saw? There were people who were laughing, crying, singing. Some were big folks; some were little ones; there were all sorts of people from everywhere, and 'Hands across America' held them all together." Even today when you mention "Hands across America," the picture of that line and the starving people of Africa come to mind.

As you talk *with* your teen, be sure to listen to the responses; this should be a two-way conversation. Invite your teen to offer other instances where music consciously or perhaps (at the time) unconsciously affected him. Ask how he felt, how he acted, or wanted to act.

Music is used frequently in advertising. Have you ever noticed how a baby or young child will stop an activity to listen to a musical TV or radio commercial? An adult driving to work or working around the house may never pay attention to the radio programs being played, but sometimes he may catch himself humming or whistling the melody of a catchy tune connected with a commercial. This music is carefully selected and executed. Much time, effort, and money is invested to produce just the right kind of music to grab the attention of the listener and to help associate a particular product with a particular sound. It is meant to be remembered and specifically in connection with a particular product.

While on the subject of influence, you might want to talk about the nonmusical influence rock might have on your young person. You might discuss fashions. Not all of our teens dress "far out," but have you noticed how music personalities can affect styles?

Hair styles have often been a point of friction between parents and their offspring since the early days of rock 'n' roll and maybe before that. This difference of taste and opinion even inspired a rock musical that was popular around 1970—*Hair*—which came to America from England.

While there is nothing morally wrong with wearing bizarre hairstyles or faddish styles of clothing, many parents (grandparents, aunts, uncles, teachers, too!) find them disturbing for a number of reasons. A parent may feel embarrassed by a teen's dress, especially when the parent senses his friends are judging him on the basis of appearance. Imitating a dress style or code of another is considered an endorsement of that person. Some of the values and ideals that rock groups represent conflict with Christian standards. Many rock entertainers are identified with drugs. Many are living together out of marriage. It bothers us when our children seem to advertise a life-style that is in direct conflict with what we support and with the standards of St. Paul, "Conduct yourselves in a manner worthy of the gospel of Christ"(Phil. 1:27). Perhaps you have tried to convince your teens that a non-Christian life-style and dress code is a poor witness for the Gospel of Jesus Christ.

Perhaps you've tried talking to your teen about this before, and it may be that you will have several conversations about this again. Appearance—hair, clothing, makeup—can be a touchy subject, but we can use appearance questions as opportunities to build a closer relationship within our family, rather than to cause a break. The first step is prayer, your personal prayer; and when you sit down to talk with your teen, begin with prayer. Ask that the Lord would guide you and build up your relationship. Ask for patience and understanding. Ask for forgiveness, and be sure to give thanks for the blessings that God has given each of you in one another. (The blessings are there even if it takes some digging to find them!)

Think about the specific time when you will talk with your teen. Find a time that is convenient for both of you, and set a definite time to meet. Keep the appointment. Meet where you will not be interrupted, where both of you feel comfortable, and where neither will feel threatened. Since you own the problem, that is, you are bothered by the appearance of your teen, you will want to send a message such as "I really feel embarrassed about the way you wear your hair (the style of clothes you wear, etc.)." You are expressing how you feel. Notice you did not say, "You embarrass me. Your hair looks like you put it through a mixer. Did you lose your comb?" Such statements are hostile and could irritate or deeply hurt your child, cause several more roadblocks to conversation, a breach in your relationships, and result in two angry parties not communicating positively. Remember what Saint Paul said about provoking your child! Let your teen respond to your statement of feeling. Together explore your feelings, and the feelings of your teen.

What feelings are involved? While you may feel embarrassed by the appearance of your teen, he would feel like an outcast if he didn't look like his peers. Ask your teen what he would suggest to resolve the problem of your conflicting viewpoints. Be sure to listen to suggestions and consider them. Look at the pros and cons. Be aware of the feelings of your teen, but also let your teen know how you feel.

If necessary, you might suggest that a less dramatic adaptation of style would be more acceptable to you and him. Talk about what is appropriate dress at any given time. Work at coming to a mutual agreement. That may come in stages with each party working out mutual agreements at different times. Expect that as your teen matures, his tastes will probably change so that appearance may be an issue only for a few years. (Could it be that *your* appearance may bother your teen? This may come up also. Be prepared and think of how you will respond—not react—to this.)

Perhaps you feel concerned rather than embarrassed. "I feel concerned about the way you appear. When you dress like 'Kiss,' you are making a statement—even without knowing it—about your values. I am concerned about that." It may be that your teen has never thought about value systems, let alone *his* value system, your value system, or the value system of a rock group as expressed by the music, dress, manner, and even the life-styles of the group members off stage. Use this opportunity to explore value systems. You now can touch on what the different rock groups might advocate. Use this opportunity to witness about Jesus. You might consider the question "Would you take Jesus to a rock concert? Why or why not?"

You, as a parent, might answer this question also. If you are inclined to keep Jesus from the rock concert, read Matt. 9:9–13.

After Jesus told Matthew to "Follow Me," Matthew invited Jesus to his home for dinner along with some of his friends who were "tax collectors and sinners." When the Pharisees condemned Jesus for eating with these tax collectors and sinners, Jesus said, "It is not the healthy who need a doctor, but the sick . . . For I have not come to call the righteous, but sinners." On the other hand, in Eph. 5:8–11 Saint Paul reminds us, "Live as children of light (for the fruit of the light consists in all goodness, righteousness and truth) and find out what pleases the Lord. Have nothing to do with the fruitless deeds of darkness, but rather expose them." Should you allow your teen to witness at a rock concert or insist he stay away from possible trouble?

Perhaps you might attend a type of rock concert together. About a year or so ago on a warm July evening, we went to a Beach Boys concert in a park. By the time we had arrived at the park, thousands of people had settled into their respective grassy areas. Local rock groups were the pre-Beach Boys entertainment, and they were going at it loud and strong. We claimed a square of grass about a city block and a half from the stage. Down by the stage a huge beach ball was being bounced around. People were having fun. Since this was a first experience in attending this kind of gathering, we were interested, curious, and out for a good time also. My son and I decided to explore the area closer to the stage. As we walked through the crowds, we noticed different types of people. As we moved closer to the stage, there were fewer children and many more teens, young adults, and adults in their late twenties to early thirties. It was warm and you could tell these people had been in the park for a while.

At first glance it seemed that everyone was having a great time. People were dancing, singing, and drumming on containers. Others were playing with the beach ball, bouncing it from group to group. There were bodies lying on the ground. Some were out cold. Beer cans and bottles were scattered here and there. People were staring off into space with no awareness of what was happening around them, some just looking, some swaying back and forth. My son asked the obvious question, "What's wrong with them?" At one point we saw several people being removed by the police. Ours was not a true rock-concert experience, though many of elements of a rock concert were present, but it was a taste of what one could be.

In spite of all of the negatives that were present, as a family we had a pleasant experience. Many of the local rock groups were good. We laughed as we became part of the "pass the giant beach ball" game. We tapped our feet to the rhythm of the music and danced along with the thousands around us. We enjoyed being a part of the group, yet set apart.

We gathered much for conversation afterward: the music and the groups performing, the people, the drinking, and the drugs. We talked about our part in the experience. Your teen may be at the stage where he prefers you to walk 10 steps behind him at the shopping mall and would "die" if you suggested tagging along to a rock concert. But perhaps you could find a compromise solution, such as some of the open-air concerts, which you could both attend, getting the same experience, but not sitting together. You could agree on rules ahead of time and after the event exchange your feelings about the event.

The arts tend to mirror society. Generally art forms reflect culture though they are a particular artist's impressions and interpretations of a segment of that society and its view of life. In a novel the characters, the script, the action, and the plot itself may mirror the daily life, the spirit, and culture in general. Photography may capture the emotions of an activity. A poem may concisely interpret a happening and state an impression. A sculpture provides a three-dimensional visualization of a thought or occurrence. Although there are those who do not consider rock an art form (merely noise, not music,), it does fulfill all art form requirements to varying degrees.

According to one view, the reason that the civil rights movement of the 1960s and 1970s succeeded is that the rock music of white Americans reflected the themes of black music. Another view is that the music of the 1960s, like all art, simply expressed the culture of the day—the sociological, legal, emotional happenings and upheaval. In any case, what is rock music saying to our youth today? Is it advocating a way of life contrary to that of the Christian? Is it a mirror of the society of today? Need we be concerned about the words or lyrics that our teens are hearing but presumably "not listening" to?

The words to some of the current hits may be (1) a mirror of the society in which our teens are growing up, (2) a source from which our teens derive their value systems, and (3) fortunately, an opportunity to deepen the relationship with our teens as we talk with them about something that interests them.

Begin by listening to some rock music so the sounds become familiar to you. (No, you do not have to have the volume on loud; put it on medium. Yes, part of the magic of rock is the volume. It hardly sounds like rock on low.) Then start listening for words. Next go to a local music store. Find the charts that tell what the top 40 hits of the day are. Purchase a copy of the sheet music for a couple of these hits or ask the manager if you may copy the words from the music. (Be sure to explain your purpose in doing this.) Use the words as a basis for discussion with your teen. Find out what's going on in life from the "rocker's" point of view.

You might begin, "I've been listening to some rock music lately. (If your teen looks at you as if you've lost your mind, smile and reassure him you're fine, not insane, just interested in him and his world.) I couldn't understand the words to some of it, so I bought some of the music. Are you familiar with these?" Share the sheet music or words with your teen. "Do you like them? What do you think about them?" The first reaction to any music is probably to the sound. "What do you think this music says? Why? How do you feel about that? Do the words concern you? How? Why? Were you familiar with the words? Do you think you learned them from listening to the music even if you weren't paying attention to the words?"

Almost any rock song will tell you something about the world in which we live. The first statement will probably express how fast-paced everything is (20th century is yesterday), including relationships (give me a moment). Look at the relationship. Is there care, concern, giving, sharing, loving? It seems to be pretty one sided (give *me* a moment, I need you *I'm* not sleeping, *I'm* lonely). What is it that the "I" of the song wants? Look at the words. The point of much of the music seems to be sexual gratification. Is there any concern for the consequences of this kind of relationship? Even a hint?

A casual sexual relationship outside of marriage is a common theme in rock music. After looking at dozens of songs, that seems to be a primary theme—self-gratification—no commitment.

Talking *with* your teen about this can lead into subjects such as our responsibilities to one another, about commitments, about marriage, about family relationships now and later. Remember to bring God into your conversation. (You did pray before your conversation, together, didn't you?) Some references might be the Old Testament books of Ruth and Song of Solomon. Proverbs deals with "words to live by" in many relational situations. The relationship between Jesus and His people, between Jesus and you, can serve as an example—relationships characterized by love, care, concern, and commitment. You might together go over the meaning of the Sixth Commandment in Luther's Catechism. (Look at the first chapter in this volume for suggestions for your talk.) The last few chapters of the Book of John, beginning with chapter 13, show especially how Jesus felt about the relationships of His people. Why not base your family devotions around these chapters? Talk about the different kinds of love. What does it mean to love, to be in love, to be loving? Look at 1 Corinthians 13 together. Ask questions to get everyone thinking, and wait for answers. Silence can indicate thinking. Be sure to encourage responses from your young people. Don't force your ideas on them, but do state what you think needs to be heard.

A suggestion for a start might be, "Let's look at some relationships in the Bible." Read Ruth together; there are only four chapters. Ask, "What kind of relationship did Ruth and Boaz have? How did it begin? How did it grow? How did they treat each other? Was their relationship one sided? Was it a selfish relationship? Caring?" Look at the other suggested readings and talk about them in the same manner. Help one another to see what God intended for our lives together in Him.

If you have a family where everyone seems to be going in a thousand directions at once, you may have to schedule a family night just to find time together. This could be a real fun evening where you can plan on listening to favorite rock tapes, videos, records, and CDs. Encourage everyone to participate. You might prepare some special food or order a pizza. Everyone should be comfortable. If you feel inclined to learn the latest dance, have your teen show you how. Part of your time together should be a discussion of some of the things that have been mentioned. Bring out the words. Talk about the groups. Discuss the relationship of volume to rock and maybe even agree on a volume setting. You might close with a study of the words and message of a Christian rock number. Be sure to check it out ahead of time to see what it has to say and then relate the message to a specific Bible reference.

Much money has been invested in rock music and related spin-offs. It takes money to keep up with the styles and changes, with the purchase of videos, tapes, and records, as well as equipment on which to play them. When requests for money for one of these items is made, what a wonderful moment—no, not to lecture on the value of money and hard work—to talk *with* your teen about using God's gifts, about budgeting, about being a good caretaker, and a thoughtful steward. How are you going to do this?

In our household recently our preteen asked for a stereo cassette player with AM-FM stereo radio for a birthday gift. That was a discussion opener. Since it was an item about which we knew little, we decided to explore the stores together to check on the costs involved, the kinds of equipment available, and the care it would require—a meaningful experience for both. As we weighed the pros and cons of various items, we talked cost—why one item was more expensive than another, initial outlay, continued care (batteries, etc.), and possible replacement costs. We talked about what we could afford and why that amount. We discussed our material blessings and being able to afford one item rather than another. After making a tentative selection, we went through a similar process with tapes. With each trip to the stores we built on our conversations, learned more about good stewardship, and above all, learned to communicate. We wondered how our preteen could earn money for the tapes? If he was earning money, could all of it go for tapes or other material things? How did proportionate giving to the Lord fit into the money plans?

What about Christian rock music? Is it better or worse than secular rock? (You may want to ask, Is it any quieter than secular rock?) Christian rock music sounds the same as secular rock. It becomes Christian when it has Christian or Biblical themes. As with any music, you need to make your judgments based on what you like to hear. What sounds do you find interesting and stimulating? Do the words express what you believe? Do they have to express what you believe for you to listen? Do you use the same criteria for listening to Christian rock as you do for other music?

If you have not listened to Christian rock, and if you (or more particularly your teen) think it's "uncool" because it's rock with "Christian" in front of it, go to a local store that sells Christian rock, probably a Christian bookstore, and do some listening. These groups are professional, and their sound is just as rock as the music of the non-Christian rock groups. The sounds and styles vary as much in Christian rock as they do in secular rock. The difference is in the lyrics.

Some of the different sounds of rock are heavy metal, New Wave, and mainstream rock. Christian rock groups fall into these kinds of sounds also. Some of the popular groups performing both live in concert and on recordings are Stryper, White Cross, Barren Cross, and Bloodgood, who are into heavy metal sounds. If you want New Wave, there's Undercover and Altar Boys (not to be confused with Alter Boys, who definitely are not Christian). Petra and Allies are two groups who are more mainstream. Most of these groups are not heard over the popular rock radio stations or found in most music stores because they do not record on secular labels. Stryper is an exception, recording on a popular label. I mention these, not as an endorsement, but because, if you are not into rock and particularly Christian rock, you may want some guidance as to what groups to look for when you're out listening and buying.

Do listen to them discriminately. Listen with your teen. Ask questions. Discuss themes. Discuss message. Discuss image. What is being stated? How is it being said? What is the effect? How does the group look? Are they different because they are Christian? Is this important? Is it OK? Do you feel comfortable listening to the group? Do you feel comfortable about letting your teen listen to the group—with or without you?

The opposite of the religious record is the satanic, occult, and cult music. (Because these topics are covered in another chapter, they are just mentioned here.) You might talk to your teen in terms of this kind of music when you talk to him about cults and the occult. It was encouraging for me to learn that many of the music stores will not stock their shelves with what they termed "questionable" music. Fortunately, many stores voluntarily decline to sell some kinds of music to younger teens and preteens. You may want to check the policies of the music stores in your area.

The music video seems to bring with it the concerns not only of rock music, but all the intellectual, emotional, and moral concerns of television. When a teen says he listens to rock, but doesn't comprehend the words, that's one thing. But when a teen sits in front of a screen, hears lyrics a parent may find alarming, and, additionally, sees images which may even cause Dad to blush, the situation is critical.

How do you handle this? Tear the video out of the VCR, throw it in the trash, and burn it? Kick in the TV screen? You could feel that way, but as you talk to your teen about any issue, you want to prepare the foundation for lifelong decision making. You want to help your teen develop a value system based on your Christ-centered beliefs. Although much of your value system is absorbed without conscious effort on the part of your teen, and much of this is transmitted without any thought by you as you go about your every day living, there comes a time to verbalize. Rock music and its spin-offs provide an opening for discussing values. Rather than eliminate the offending video completely without any consideration, find out first what your teen is thinking. To ban it from your home does not ban it from the home of one of his friends. You want to prepare your teen for making decisions. In this case, to watch or not to watch, that is the question.

You might begin, "I see you're watching music videos. Do you mind if I watch with you?" Some teens might get up and leave when you sit down. You may have to be prepared for that. How will you handle that? Will you sit there alone and watch a music video? Will you find out why the teen left? Remember the Ephesians 6 passage. It may take some "active listening." "You feel threatened when I want to watch music videos with you." Or, it may be that "You feel embarrassed" or perhaps "You feel offended." Find out what your teen is feeling and deal with that before you get into the rock video.

If your teen says, "Sure. Why not," sit and experience the video. You may have to carefully calculate the timing of the discussion. If your teen is absorbed in the music, questions or comments will bounce right off. Wait for an appropriate time to interrupt, such as the end of a selection, and say, "Can we talk about what we just saw? What do you think about it?" Maybe it will be the fast-paced changing of scenes that appeals, the way the music and the visuals move together. Perhaps it is the music alone, and the images on the screen are just "there." Maybe it's the entertainers who are appealing. Find out what your teen likes. Find out why. Talk about the message the videos convey. What do they actually say? What do they suggest? How does this fit into what God says? Does the message, both stated and implied, contradict what you as God's child believe and live? How? Why or why not? What do you think you should do about it? What would God want you to do about it? Maybe you should pose the question asked earlier about rock concerts. "Would you watch this (or any) music video with Jesus?"

Rock music, as all things, must be measured by our value system. For the Christian, Christ is in the center of that system. For the Christian parent, the responsibility of training the child includes sharing Jesus and the way of life He showed His children. Rock music—use it! Use it to communicate *with* your teen. Share time with him. Share with him concepts that are important to you. Talk *with* him. Listen to him. If rock music is a part of his world, it is a part of your world. Use it as a bridge to your teen and a bridge to his future. Help him to learn how to make decisions based on the values you have as a redeemed, chosen child of God.

Points to Remember

1. Begin with prayer for guidance and direction!
2. The rock music of the 1980s is not the rock of the 1950s. The mood and the message have changed.
3. Music does exercise a visible influence on us. Church music, commercial music, mood music are all carefully chosen for the influence they exercise.
4. Many fads such as those in hairstyle and clothing are based on how rock stars appear and dress—showing the influence they have.

5. While clothing may be free from social messages and meaning, the dress of many rock stars makes statements which are not in keeping with a Christian witness.
6. Consider attending a rock concert to experience firsthand what occurs. Use the opportunity to share with your teen and provide a solid witness to your faith. Witness! Don't moralize!
7. Examine carefully the words from rock songs and discuss them as a springboard for sharing your Christian values, commitment, and what it means to be responsible.
8. Become familiar with Christian rock to see if it is an acceptable alternative for you and your teen.

Counterfeit Religion in The Light

Bruce Frederickson

$\mathcal{F}$or many people the word *cult* conjures up ominous and illusory images. Some confuse *cult* with *occult*.

A cult is an organization, religious in nature, that often begins as an offshoot of some larger religious group and continues with great enthusiasm, for the purpose of promoting a certain belief, leader, or both. The new group usually separates from the main organization because of a difference in teaching or authority.

On the other hand, *occult* is a Latin word which means *secret* or *hidden*. In Christian circles occult has come to refer to the practices of fortune-telling, black magic and spiritism. The next chapter deals with the occult as a separate topic.

Ours Is a Nation of Joiners!

"Pastor? Our son Tom just called from college. It was his first weekend, and already he has made some friends. They have invited him to a retreat. It's a Christian group. They plan to spend the weekend up in the mountains helping delinquent teens find their way in life. I feel so good about what he is doing!"

"Pastor? Tom phoned us again. That retreat he went on last weekend—it seems that they felt he was so successful they wanted him to stay another week. It sounds like he's doing such a fine job . . . I hope he doesn't neglect his own community!"

"Pastor? Do you know anything about this group our Tom joined? It's called Creative Christian Community. I can't seem to find a phone number or address for it. I'm worried. His roommate said he hasn't been back to the dorm since that first weekend. We've been thinking of calling the police."

"Pastor? Would you pray for Tom and for us? The local authorities told us that this group called the Creative Christian Community has probably kidnapped our son. Yet they say there's nothing we can do about it. He's 18, and he went with them of his own free will! I'm scared, Pastor!"

"Pastor? Our Tom called us today. It's been two months since he went to college. He informed us that he has dropped out of school and has joined this . . . this group of his. He spoke about how much good they are doing for humanity—and that he wants us to send his savings. What do you think we should do? He sounded so strange, so distant. It's as though it's not our Tom anymore!"

Our country, if not the world, is undergoing a renewed interest in religious and spiritual matters. While most traditional churches aren't experiencing a corresponding increase in membership, the renewed interest is immediately apparent in several other ways. Sales of books and magazines dealing with so-called spiritual matters are skyrocketing. Distinctive *Christian* bookstores have sprung up in many communities. Large bookstores in large cities report a rapid turnover of material in their religion, philosophy, and occult sections.

People are curious. People want to know more, especially about those things they can't see. All of us want to know where we came from, our roots, where we are going, our destiny! Literally hundreds of self-styled professionals crisscross the country, speaking and writing on topics ranging from a new worldwide unification of

Christianity to a *harmonic convergence* of the planets. They attract audiences of various sizes and often receive substantial gifts of money and property to enable them to carry out their work.

Well-known radio and television personalities promote their own brand of spirituality through seminars, books, and magazine articles. Some unknown personalities have become popular and famous almost overnight as they talk about such diverse things as world peace through concentration and reincarnation, or getting it right the next time around.

Ours is a country of joiners. Many Americans are willing to become a part of almost any organization, promoting any cause. When it comes to religion, the enthusiasm seems to be the greatest! Judging by the millions of dollars required to operate these powerful organizations, people are also willing to invest some of their wealth as well.

Our young people are seen as an easy target for groups like this. Young people are highly impressionable and often quite idealistic and hopeful about the future of our world. They need so much to have something to believe in. Some groups, called cults, operating under the guise of legitimate religion, are kidnapping and brainwashing thousands of young people each year. As parents, you have a right to be concerned. What can you do?

What's the Problem?

Newspapers in the 1960s and 1970s were full of horror stories. Young people, usually of college age, simply disappeared. Often when they turned up a short time later, they were safe, but not sound. They had become committed members of cults. These cults were labeled dangerous, not only because the doctrines they taught were questionable, but also because of their practices in recruiting and keeping members.

Charges of brainwashing were leveled against cultic leaders. Often counterchanges were filed against parents when their attempts at kidnapping their children out of the cult failed. Yet many young people who were kidnapped and successfully deprogrammed came out of these groups with all the zeal of someone who had quit smoking or drinking. These young people told horror stories of being deprived of sleep and nutrition. They admitted that they had been enticed into the group through deception. Once in the group, they were subjected to subtle but highly effective coercion. Often they were made to feel guilty or ashamed. Under constant scrutiny, they were never left alone.

Someone who hasn't walked for months needs to relearn the walking process all over again. Similarly, former members complained of great difficulty in thinking and making decisions for themselves. Even after leaving, they complained of harassment by former friends in the cult. Many were pressured to rejoin.

Concerned parents gathered into groups to support one another in their loss, expressing hope that they could effectively warn other parents of the perils of cult involvement. Many parents were willing to do almost anything to rescue their children from what they perceived as extremely dangerous psychological situations.

Perhaps you are a parent, wondering what cults really are. With young people in your home or away at school, you may wonder if they are vulnerable to the devious tricks of cult recruiters. Perhaps your child will receive an interesting invitation as Tom did at the beginning of the chapter. Maybe you remember only too well the disillusionment that some young people feel toward religion, and you fear for your own children.

You may just want to inform yourself about the problem and help ease the dangers. Think back to when you were a teenager. What was most important? What occupied most of your time? When you were upset, what happened to your relationship with those usually closest and most supportive of you? Did the bond become stronger, or was it often strained? To whom did you turn for support?

Listen to the words of Paul to Timothy: "For the time will come when men will not put up with sound doctrine. Instead, to suit their own desires, they will gather around them a great number of teachers to say what their itching ears want to hear. They will turn their ears away from the truth and turn aside to myth" (2 Tim. 4:3–5).

Have you ever feared such a thing in your family? Then read on! "But you, keep your head in all situations, endure hardship, do the work of an evangelist, discharge all the duties of your ministry" (4:5). As an evangelist, a bringer of God's Good News, be especially sensitive to the needs of those in your own family. Remember, your Savior, Jesus, holds you and your family in the center of His will!

Churches and Cults Have Changed!

In the years since the questionable recruiting techniques of cults were first uncovered, several things have changed both within the cults, and in the way others view them. But the danger that cults pose to Christian families still exists. As Christian parents, we must be forewarned and thus forearmed!

Literally hundreds of books have been written about cults. Some expose individual cults, such as the Jehovah's Witnesses or the Unification Church, known as the Moonies. Others deal with the coercive activities of all cults in general.

Cults have changed, too! They have revised their defenses. Rather than operate under a cloak of secrecy and intrigue, some cults have opened their meeting places to the public. They welcome visits by the public and angry parents alike. Some groups have invited prominent Christian clergy to all-expense-paid seminars in attractive locations such as Bermuda or Japan. Cults are seeking to legitimatize their existence alongside other evangelical Christian groups across the country.

But in all honesty, we must admit that cults have done great harm to the Christian church. The assault of cults upon Christian families has forced church leaders and members alike to ask themselves some rather painful questions. Cult recruitment is effective because the Christian church has left voids that cults easily identify and turn to their own profit. As a parent, you will want to consider how cults can attack your family. Take a hard look and discover if there are voids which you or your church have failed to fill.

Cult Madness

Many denominations were scrambling to find and fill these voids when, in the early morning hours of November 15, 1978, stories of a gigantic nightmare began to filter out of the steamy jungles of Guyana, a small, developing country on the northern coast of South America. Jim Jones, a U.S. citizen and an officially registered American clergyman in a rather large United States Christian denomination, had convinced nearly 1,000 people to follow him to the forbidding jungles of South America. There Jones led followers to build an experimental agricultural community in which they could live more freely.

According to first reports, Jones had simply suggested that his followers commit mass suicide as a protest to investigations being made into the way he ran his community. However, circumstances surrounding that fateful night have caused many to question how freely these people died. How could one man convince so many people to do things that were otherwise contrary to their own free will? Many parents were haunted by such questions as, What if it had been my child who lay down to die in that remote jungle that night? What if it had been my kid who freely drank Jones' poison-laced drink mix to join his protest against dangers which existed only in his psychotic mind? How could a thousand people do such a foolish and horrible thing?

Who Is Vulnerable?

Many young people in our country today are exposed to the deceptive recruiting practices of the modern cults—new religious groups pouring out love and concern for young people who desperately need friendship and acceptance. Often too late, the new recruit learns that this love is conditional upon performing in an accepted manner.

Recruiters for these dangerous cults look for people who are between 17 and 29 years of age, intelligent, with a serious outlook on life, idealistic about social issues, already members of some established religious group, and facing a change in life.

Some who have come out of cults have suggested that the most profitable recruitment time is the first two weeks of classes on a college campus or the last two weeks before graduation.

New students are often friendless, looking for someone or something as support. They are lonely. An invitation, any invitation, is readily welcomed and accepted.

Soon-to-be graduates face many difficult decisions for the first time in their lives. They are looking for someone to tell them what to do. Graduation can be a nightmare, with bills to pay, jobs to find and a place to stay. Cults often meet these needs immediately, and so gain converts to their cause.

Jesus Is the Real Thing!

The American Bankers Association conducts a two-week seminar to help bank tellers detect and identify counterfeit currency. It is interesting to note that, for the first 10 or so days of this very popular workshop, participants handle nothing but the real thing. The theory is that they cannot identify fake currency until they are totally familiar with real bills.

Similarly, before you, as a parent, tackle the counterfeit new religions, you must be completely familiar with true religion. As you talk to your teens with a possible interest if not actual involvement in counterfeit religions, it is imperative that you both work with the same set of definitions!

Christianity is not simply a set of rules to live by. Neither is it a crutch to shore up brokenness. Christianity realistically recognizes the common human predicament: The first humans lost their first state of perfection and broke their relation with God. To be sure, Jesus Christ died on a cross as our substitute, as John 3:16 puts it: "God so loved the world that He gave His one and only Son, that whoever believes in Him shall not perish but have eternal life." Nevertheless, ours is still a fallen world, and every aspect of the plant, animal, and geophysical world has been tainted by the fall. Even the mind and the will of man is turned away from God. That explains the existence of the cults, as well as all evil in the world. Faith in Jesus as the Redeemer—faith which itself is a gift of God—is the only resource for alleviating the problems and combatting the forces of evil. Most important for understanding life, because of Jesus our rebellion against God has been forgiven; we are now liberated; our sins are forgiven; and we are free to live a life in service to God. There is nothing that anyone can do to earn, deserve or merit forgiveness of sins and eternal life. God offers it only one way—freely as a gift.

But what if someone from a cult approaches you or the young people in your family? Perhaps one has already knocked on your door. What will you do? What will you say?

Decide that you will talk only about worthwhile things (Phil. 4:8). Don't get caught in the trap of running other religions down. Decide that when you talk to others about religion, your conversation will center on Jesus Christ and what He has done for all people (1 Cor. 2:2). It is easy to become sidetracked on some other issue. That is exactly what a cult recruiter wants.

Many of the cults are not really new. They simply pick up and continue a false doctrine which has existed for centuries. But how do you identify the false ones?

"Dear friends, do not believe every spirit, but test the spirits to see whether they are from God, because many false prophets have gone out into the world. This is how you can recognize the Spirit of God: Every spirit . . . that does not acknowledge Jesus is not from God," (1 John 4:1-3).

In order to test the spirits, we have to know the real thing, what the Spirit of God has said. Pay particular attention to what the other religion says about Jesus Christ. Don't simply ask whether this new religion admits that a real flesh and blood person named Jesus ever lived. Satan can do that, too. Ask followers of that religion whether they believe that God came into the flesh as Jesus who then died as a sacrifice for the sins of the world. According to the Scriptures, that is why Christ came to earth.

In testing the spirits, the key is what do you think about the Christ? (Matt. 22:42). Jesus Himself asked that question of some Jews who had tried to trick Him. Actually, Jesus asks the same question of followers of all religions and of us, too, "What do you think of the Christ?"

Let people see Jesus in all His glory, and simplicity. Share with them a simple Bible verse, such as John 3:16, and what it means to you to know with certainty that because of Jesus' death and resurrection you have eternal life as a free gift.

Too Good to Be True

"When you meet the friendliest people you have ever known, who introduce you to the most loving group of people you've ever encountered, and you find the leader to be the most inspired, caring, compassionate and understanding person you've ever met, and then you learn that the cause of the group is something you never dared to hope could be accomplished, and all of this sounds too good to be true—it probably is too good to be true. Don't give up your education, your hopes and ambitions to follow a rainbow" (Jeanne

Milles, a survivor of Jonestown, as quoted in a tract from Free Minds, Box 4216, Minneapolis, Minn. 55414, 612/376-2528).

Have you ever discovered something which was too good to be true? Perhaps at the time you thought you were dreaming. Many who have been involved with cults return with similar stories and are thankful to have escaped alive from the dream that became a nightmare.

How Do New Religions Begin?

Most cults are launched by an individual. This person may have begun with a noble purpose, such as helping people, or with the hope of fooling people and gaining popularity. Cults often choose a single goal or theme such as world peace, or the elimination of problems between people. By making very attractive promises, the bait is often taken before the individual realizes what is happening.

The reason cults have flourished in our country over the past 20 years are many, growing out of problems, such as hunger, unemployment, or the threat of war and annihilation. The problems persist despite massive attempts to overcome them. An informational blitz is burying the world in knowledge while at the same time more efficient and faster communication systems are shrinking a world that is threatened with ecological and nuclear problems leading to self-destruction. While uncertainty about jobs plagues some, others are uncertain what to do with ever increasing amounts of leisure time.

Assaulted by change, many churches have lost their stablility. Unattended spiritual problems become spawning grounds for many of the cults. Churches are becoming more secularized. Belief in the supernatural is fading. Values once taught by the church as universal are being questioned and modified. Many young people perceive that, while churches talk a good line, older Christians in leadership positions are doing little to reduce the burning social issues facing the *now* generation.

With the packaging of religion for specific audiences, people of all ages are confused with what *church* is.

God, in Christ, has come to our world with an eternal message. We may change and the world around us may change, but God never changes. We always have the same need for forgiveness and salvation. As long as we keep our eyes on Jesus, we can be sure that we are looking in the right direction. But we must constantly be on our guard. Even the educated are not immune to the lure of cults. Be forewarned and forearmed by staying close to Him, studying His Word, and speaking to Him regularly in prayer!

What Do Cults Offer?

Cults are usually attractive because they seem to offer something new. Paul warned of people whose ears would be itching to hear something new (2 Tim. 4:3). Cults thrive on these desires. Cultic leaders may offer new teachings, a new life-style, a new identity, new freedom, or a new source of authority. For many, "the old, old story of Jesus and His love" is outdated. For example, Jehovah's Witnesses deny hell and talk of a new heaven and a new earth. The Moonies promote a new Messiah who makes our Savior obsolete.

Nearly all religious cults are built around a single individual, usually the founder, usually a strong, dynamic leader, who projects the image of a father figure. Quite frequently, the leader claims to be God—or at least a Messiah. Such strong, seductive leaders are often able to convince blind followers that they are the source of true wisdom.

Describing the rest of the world as evil and degenerate, cultic leaders invite recruits into their paradise, promising relief from all the problems of the world. They attract many, young and old.

Cults exploit the normal needs of young people who are approaching the age of independence, weary of religious limitations and rebelling against parental supervision. They may jump at the chance to be "really free." Cultic leaders offer freedom, but it is a trap. The freedom is sticky, and it isn't free. It is like a fishing hook—it has a barb! Watch out!

Cultic leaders separate their flock from the rest of the world by removing them from others physically, or at the very least, informationally. They often set up a strict hierarchy with themselves at the top, claiming to possess the only true authority. These new masters make promises to recruits and occasionally are able to deliver on some of them—until the hook is set. By then it is too late.

A cult can be identified by the strict control imposed on members. New recruits are deprived of sleep, nourishing food, and well-balanced meals. After a period of time under such treatment, cult members tend to be quite compliant. If your young people are involved with a group you suspect to be a cult, listen carefully to what they say about the group and its leader!

One young cult dropout admitted joining a very idealistic group. He was impressed with its goals. Not until he had been with the group for 10 days, did he hear the name of the main leader. Although he expressed disappointment with the leader, he had made an emotional commitment. "By that time it was too late. I was hooked!" He later admitted that not one of the goals was ever met. In fact, once the recruits were committed, the goals were completely discarded.

Many want immediate answers to questions and are short on patience. Cultic leaders feed on that impatience. After a brief conversation, recruiters often can discover the key that unlocks a person's defenses. They counter with immediate answers!

Recall your own youthful idealism, and you may understand when your teenager becomes disillusioned with the world as he perceives it, if he feels that the answers and solutions offered by his parents and teachers are inadequate. Cultic leaders know human nature and can exploit this idealism. They readily offer solutions for hunger or joblessness, but unfortunately, they are almost always empty and totally deceptive.

The promises of the cults sound good until you have invested so much of yourself emotionally that it is too late to back out. To the lonely they offer companionship; to the poor, money; to the sick or suffering, healing. While churches are good at laying guilt on young people, the cults attract new members by promising relief from such guilt—and simply by joining. To some this appears to be grace, as in Christianity. Nothing could be further from the truth. If any religion offers forgiveness which is not based on the shed blood of Jesus Christ, it is false.

Ah, but There's a Catch!

Once the bait is taken, recruits discover that cults make requirements of them, too. Cults always require a sacrifice. Usually this involves interrupting an education or career. Often it means giving up family. They may misquote Scripture to back up their claims (Matt. 10:35–39). Cults also require an investment—usually of time and money. As the relationship with the cult grows so does the investment until it is total and nearly impossible to dissolve. Minds become sluggish and follow directions blindly. After coming out of cults, some young people report that their thinking seems stiff and stodgy, like an automobile which hasn't started in years.

Cults are very jealous of other relationships. They invariably require a renunciation of all past commitments, especially to family and friends. Once a recruit has renounced former relationships, there is no choice but to establish a close communion with the new group. Cults teach transcendence—that the group is more important than the individual who becomes lost in the multitude. This is how they justify a denial of self, including pleasures, and ultimately all bodily needs.

Fight Fire with Fire!

The only way to deal with a cult is to confront the issues head on. No amount of arguing will convince anyone, unless the argument is based on God's Word and is accompanied by God's Spirit.

The best way to deal with a person who is vulnerable to a cult or has already been approached or recruited is to listen politely to what the cult has to say and then ask the same courtesy of them. Center your comments on what the Bible says about Jesus Christ and His blood-bought forgiveness for the sins of the world. Invite the cult members to consider what you have said, and tell them you will pray for them.

The teachings of cults are like a fire which consumes everything in its path. There is only one sure way to deal with a cult: Use the fire of the Holy Spirit. Speak God's Word of truth about Jesus Christ. Point cult members to Jesus' death on the cross for their sin. Share with them the certainty you have of your forgiveness and eternal life. By all means leave the door open for further conversation. Pray for them.

What Can You Do?

Many parents have confessed that, when confronted with cultic involvement, their first mistake was to become defensive. Not to become defensive requires self-discipline. If you perceive that your child's freedom is being endangered, becoming defensive is automatic.

Remember, young people involved with a cult may have been brainwashed. Their decisions, their speech, and their actions may not be their own. Do not reject or condemn these people. Assure them of your unconditional love. Make every effort to educate yourself about the particular group with which they are involved. Study the mind control techniques used by the particular group.

The Citizens Freedom Foundation has suggested the following Dos and Don'ts.

Do

1. Record names, addresses and phone numbers of people known to associate in any way with the group.

2. Maintain a written chronology of events associated with your child's association with the group.

3. Answer all communication from your child in sincere, firm, but unrecriminating language. Do not be excessively critical in your correspondence.

4. Collect all related items from newspapers, books, and magazines about this particular group and the subject of thought reform and mind-control techniques as practiced by cults.

5. Keep your cool. Avoid threats. Keep the lines of communication open.

6. Establish and continue an association with an organized group of parents who are faced with similar problems.

7. File a written complaint with the proper local officials.

Now the Don'ts!

1. Don't allow other siblings to visit the cult victim. They are prime targets for recruitment. It is much more difficult to recover more than one member of a family at a time!

2. Do not send money to your child or to the group. Without support the group cannot survive.

3. Do not give original documents to anyone unless required by proper law enforcement officials. Any requested documents can be photocopied!

4. Do not be persuaded by "professionals" to send large amounts of money for "treatments" or legal action until you have verified their credentials and qualifications for handling your particular problem.

5. Do not give up! Remember that your child is a product of your love, training, heredity, and home environment. These influences can never be permanently eliminated by a technique.

6. Do not feel guilty or alone. This problem is faced by thousands of parents annually. It affects families of all religious, economic, and cultural backgrounds.

The Plight of Parents

"Unless it happened to you, you can't possibly imagine the anguish of losing a son or daughter to the extremist religious cults" (Charles H. Edwards, "How I Rescued My Son from the Moonies," *Medical Economics*, Nov. 1, 1976, pp. 73–80). The average person has heard horror stories about what happened in other parts of the country and to other families. No parent can fully understand the magnitude or the seriousness of the problem until it strikes closer to home. Terms like mind control, brainwashing, and deprogramming may have little meaning until someone you know is affected!

Feelings of guilt, shame, and despair are all very common in parents whose child has joined an extremist religious group. Some parents succeed in visiting the family member who is in a cult. More often than not, cult members are prevented from seeing family members. They are purposely separated. As the incidence of kidnapping and deprogramming increases, cults tighten their security.

Cults often whisk young recruits all over the country or the world to avoid detection by parents. When they are permitted to write home, letters from these naive recruits are mailed from false locations in an attempt to throw unsuspecting parents off the trail.

Whatever you do, don't give up! You are not alone. There are other parents who are experiencing the same frustration as you are. Our God, who has done so much for us through Christ, is always with you. "Humble yourselves, therefore, under God's mighty hand, that He may lift you up in due time. Cast all your anxiety on Him because He cares for you" (1 Peter 5:7).

Resources You May Use

Parents can do many things. Perhaps most important is the sixth suggestion in both the *dos* and *don'ts* listed above. Involve yourself with a support/informational organization that can help you. Many of them can provide general information about cultic involvement; some specialize in providing information about one or several groups.

The following may be helpful:

The Commission on Organizations, The Lutheran Church—Missouri Synod, Rev. Philip Lochhaas, Executive Director, 1333 South Kirkwood Rd., Saint Louis, Mo. 63122-7295, 314/965-9000.

Spiritual Counterfeits Project, Box 4308, Berkeley, Calif. 94704, 415/548-7947.

Christian Research Institute, Walter Martin, P.O. Box 500, San Juan Capistrano, Calif. 92693.

C.M.I., Ron Carlson, 7601 Superior Terrace, Eden Prairie, Minn. 55344.

Citizens Freedom Foundation, Box 608370, Chicago, Ill. 60626, can provide you with a local branch in your area.

Cult Awareness Network, 2421 W. Pratt Blvd., Chicago, Ill. 60645.

Free Minds, Box 4216, Minneapolis, Minn. 55414, 612/376-2528.

There are also a number of excellent resources available in Christian bookstores, magazines and newspapers:

Lifton, Robert J. *Thought Reform and the Psychology of Totalism.* New York: W.W. Norton and Company, 1963.

Enroth, Ron. *The Lure of the Cults.* Downers Grove: Inter-Varsity, 1987.

—————, and J. Gordon Melton. *Why Cults Succeed Where the Church Fails.* Elgin, Ill.: Brethren Press, 1985.

Petersen, William J. *Those Curious New Cults in the '80's.* New Canaan, Conn.: Keats Publishing, 1982.

McDowell, Josh, and Don Stewart. *Understanding the Cults.* San Bernardino, Calif.: Here's Life Publishers, 1982.

Martin, Walter. *The Kingdom of the Cults.* Minneapolis, Minn: Bethany House, 1985.

Several full-length feature films also describe cult life in detail.

Both the subject of brainwashing and deprogramming are dealt with in some cases. These films are often available from your local family video store:
>   *Ticket to Heaven*
>   *Split Image*
>   *The Guyana Tragedy*

In Conclusion!

In confronting and dealing with cults, it is important to understand something of the historical, sociological, and psychological perspectives which are involved both in recruitment and life within the group.

From a Christian perspective, however, we must understand that there is another, more important consideration. The age-old struggle between God and Satan, between good and evil, is once again shown in the conflict between cults and the Christian faith (2 Cor. 2:11).

The patterns of activities described in this chapter are not isolated or accidental. Satan deliberately plans to attack people at the very center of their existence—their spirituality. His main goal is to draw people away from the religious beliefs of their youth and away from the families that would support them in these beliefs.

Long ago, the Apostle Peter warned us of Satan's goal. "Be self-controlled and alert. Your enemy the devil prowls around like a roaring lion looking for someone to devour. Resist him, standing firm in the faith" (1 Peter 5:8–9). Satan wants to devour you and your family members. Know the one in whom you believe—Jesus Christ. Know that He has claimed an eternal victory over Satan for you!

As the head of the church, Christ is the first to be attacked. You can identify which groups are not Christian by asking the simple question, "What do you think of Jesus and His death on the cross for the sins of the world?" When we are attacked, we can pray for strength, protection, and deliverance. Rely upon Ps. 50:15; Matt. 11:28; Eph. 6:11–18.

The most powerful weapons are available to you. Use the Word of God and prayer. Allow God's love to flow through you to the young people in your family. Then, with the power of His Spirit, celebrate the full life He has given you together!

Points to Remember

1. Cult recruitment is effective because Christian churches have left a void.
2. Young people who are seeking love, friendship, and acceptance are vulnerable to cults.
3. Many cults are actually based on false doctrines existing for centuries.
4. Listen carefully to how cult members testify to Jesus. Is He the Son of God? Lord and Savior? The only way to salvation?
5. Most cults are built around one central person who describes the rest of the world as bad and imposes strict controls on individual members.
6. Cults offer immediate satisfaction and appeal to a person's weak points.
7. The only way to deal with cult members is through God's Word. Fight fire with the fire of God's Word!
8. Be familiar with the list of dos and don'ts in this chapter.
9. Get information about particular cults in your area.

"Tho' Devils All the World Should Fill . . ."

Bruce Frederickson

*I*n the previous chapter *occult* was defined as *secret* or *hidden*. Actually, the word originally referred to anything that could not be grasped by the five senses. Recently *occult* has been used, especially by Christians, to describe any practice or belief in the existence and use of supernatural forces that are not from God, but are spiritual forces of Satan.

Occult is often confused with *cult*, because the words sound quite similar, and many of the new religious cults engage in practices that began in witchcraft and Satanism. Cults are satanic in that they discredit and tear down the church of Jesus Christ.

Occult can be divided into three main categories. Astrology and fortune-telling are attempts to predict future events and analyze human character. Magic or witchcraft seeks to control animate and inanimate objects and thus gain power. Spiritism is the belief that people can contact the spirits of the dead.

Recently another form of occult, called the New Age, has reared its ugly head, especially among Christians. Most Christians familiar with the Bible know that casting spells in the name of Satan is against God's will. Scripture makes it clear that God has revealed only as much of the future as He wishes us to know. But The New Age is particularly dangerous since it is vague and confusing. When popular, self-styled theologians advocate such innocent sounding things as world peace through the transformation of all people, even Christians can become confused.

In the preface to his well-known book, *The Screwtape Letters*, the famous Christian apologist C. S. Lewis says, "There are two equal and opposite errors into which our race can fall about the devils. One is to disbelieve in their existence. The other is to believe and to feel an excessive and unhealthy interest in them. They themselves are equally pleased by both errors and heal a materialist or a magician with the same delight" (New York: Macmillan, 1959, p. 3).

Those who deny the existence of invisible evil spirits, and Satan as their chief, play right into his hand, for they are denying one of the basic purposes for which our Lord came, to destroy the devil's work (1 John 3:8). Of course, Satan feels the same way about Jesus and will not hesitate to frighten Christ's followers so much that they remain weak and powerless.

Martin Luther in his famous hymn, "A Mighty Fortress Is Our God," says, "Tho' devils all the world should fill, / All eager to devour us, / We tremble not, we fear no ill, / They shall not overpow'r us. / This world's prince may still / Scowl fierce as he will, / He can harm us none, / He's judged; the deed is done; / One little word can fell him." That Word is Jesus. His death on the cross completed the sacrifice for the sins of the world (John 19:30), and the defeat of the prince of sin, Satan, was also complete.

Jesus is the Victor, yet Satan, with all his deviousness, tries to enter our lives and fool us into believing otherwise. Never forget St. Paul's words, "Having disarmed the powers and authorities, He [Jesus], makes a public spectacle of them, triumphing over them by the cross" (Col. 2:15).

If we still smart under his attacks and temptations, we need only recall that Satan is doomed and defeated. Like a chicken whose head has been cut off, he may still thrash around for a time. Actually, Satan is more like a huge dragon. He is the reptile of Revelation 12. His head has been severed and he is defeated. But thrashing in anger, his huge tail swishes back and forth trying to drag others down with him.

On the other hand, we dare not assume that Satan cannot hurt or harm us. As Corrie ten Boom says in her book, *Defeated Enemies*, (Fort Washington, Penn: Christian Literature Crusade, 1962), "The Christian life is often a battlefield and the devil has about 6,000 years of experience in laying traps for the saints." We dare not relax our guard against Satan for even one moment. Satan and his lying ways are real. We meet him in the third chapter of the Bible [Genesis], and his opposition to Christ is prominent and persistent until the third last chapter [of the Bible] where his complete destruction is described."

The Occult Explosion

In the last 20 years there has been a phenomenal explosion of interest in the occult, roughly coinciding with the release of the song, "The Age of Aquarius," by the Fifth Dimension. In the late 1960s, supermarkets and stores sold games and puzzles advertising the signs of the zodiac. People became more familiar with the sign of their birth month than with their baptism birthday. Jewelry with zodiacal signs became very popular. Astrologers, such as Jeanne Dixon, once thought to be cute, became popular household words. One Illinois daily newspaper removed its astrology column and received several thousand letters of protest in a single day!

Movies such as *Rosemary's Baby* and *The Exorcist* almost glorified Satan. People became familiar with some of his deceptive ways, and yet little was done to glorify Christ and familiarize these same people with the victory Christ had already won by the shedding of His blood.

In his books *My Name Is Legion* (Iowa West District, 1975) and *How to Respond to the Occult* (St. Louis: Concordia, 1977), David Hoover quotes from a March 1970 article in *McCall's* magazine entitled "The Occult Explosion." The statistics which Hoover revealed were shocking.

Even if only a small percentage of them were true, the article demonstrated convincingly that there has indeed been an explosion of interest in the occult; and, as when an explosion occurs, a powerful, potentially destructive force has been unleashed, frequently leaving casualties.

Several factors explain such a rapid increase in satanic activity in the past 20 years. Many of America's educated people have expressed a keen interest in Eastern religions. Some suggest that the increased interest in occult is only a yardstick measuring the emotional security of people. When people are filled with uncertainty and doubt, they cling to almost anything. Like cults, occult has a great deal of reality to it. Like cults, occult offers immediate answers. There is no question about it—it works. Satan does have power.

Perhaps most important to us Christians is that this increased interest in Satanic activities is merely a barometer, indicating the approach of the last days. Satan knows his time is short. He wants to drag as many people down with him as he can.

Since he already owns those who don't believe in Jesus, he focuses his efforts on believers. In that sense, trouble with Satanism is a compliment to Christians. The closer you are to Christ the harder Satan tries to wrestle you from Jesus' grasp. For that reason, Christians must be that much more on their guard. We must never forget the great promises of Jesus, "no one can snatch them out of my hand" (John 10:28).

As Paul warned the young minister, Timothy, "There will be terrible times in the last days" (2 Tim. 3:1). Satan will throw his best at us, and we must be prepared to stand against him. But we are not alone. Keep repeating that one little word that can and will fell him—the name of Jesus!

Parents Beware!

As a Christian parent, do not drop your guard! Recall that Satan enjoys complacent or doubting parents. The faith of every member of your family is at stake, and the young people in your home are especially vulnerable.

As one who has been charged by God to watch over the spiritual well-being of your children, be aware of the nature of the explosion, arm yourself and your family with appropriate passages from the Word of God, and stand ready to defend that faith using all the mighty power Christ offers you.

Peter warns, "be self-controlled and alert. Your enemy the devil prowls around like a roaring lion looking for someone to devour. Resist him, standing firm in the faith because you know that your brothers throughout the world are undergoing the same kind of sufferings" (1 Peter 5:8–9). "Be fully armed with the Sword of the Spirit, the mighty Word of God," (Eph. 6:17). Jesus has promised to stay close to you forever. Stay close to Him!

Satan, the Master of Deception

Because Satan is a master at deception, we must be very careful not to take him too lightly. Some laugh him off as a humorous little character wearing long red underwear, a pointed tail, and carrying a pitchfork. There is no telling what will arouse our interest in him.

One youth reported becoming interested in Satanism after reading a book. Another said after reading a magazine article the temptations became more effective. Satanic forces are invisible, able to roam and tempt people (Matt. 12:43–45). Many in number, they are powerful, and sneaky and are organized much like an army (Mark 5:9). These spiritual foot soldiers of Satan are knowledgeable about both God and people; yet they have the dubious ability to lie (James 2:19; John 8:44). Satan and his evil helpers are all evil, bent on nothing less than total destruction of Christ's kingdom (Luke 22:31; Eph. 6:12).

But knowing his name and his abilities is not enough. Scripture tells us how Satan and his evil spirits can work in the lives of people here. If we actually see him attempting to lead people away from God, we can imagine how he works on us and on our children.

Forms of the Occult

Astrology and fortune-telling, magic or witchcraft, and spiritism are the three general categories of the occult.

Astrology and fortune-telling developed over many years. After observing the movement of the stars and other heavenly bodies, primitive people attributed changes in their lives to the movement of the stars. Likewise the character of people born under certain configurations was considered set by the stars. Before the modern era, many people felt that heavenly bodies could actually control world events and human character. Therefore, predicting constellation changes was considered the key to knowing the future.

But God does not want us to know more about the future than what is revealed in the Bible (Deut. 29:29). He has already told us the most important thing about our future: If we believe in Jesus, we will live with Him forever. To desire or attempt to discover any more than that is sin.

Many people read horoscopes or use other fortune-telling techniques. While these methods have no real predictive value, Satan can use them to cause doubt about the future. The most important part of our future, our relationship with our God, is also at stake. Satan can use the power of suggestion to cause these predictions to become self-fulfilling prophecies.

In His Word, God warns against star-gazing (Deut. 4:19–20; 18:10–14). If His people wish reliable information about their future they are to ask Him in prayer, listen to Him speak in His Word, and believe.

Magick, spelled with a "k" to distinguish it from ordinary stage or sleight-of-hand magic, is dangerous. It is done with the help of Satan and his evil powers. God has also condemned these practices (Deut. 18:10–12), particularly because they are idolatrous. Power which comes from a source other than God will draw our attention away from Him who alone is the Creator and Sustainer of the universe (Ex. 20:1–4).

Jesus makes it clear that He opposes everything that Satan is for (Matt. 12:22–27). Paul includes witchcraft among sinful works of the flesh (Gal. 5:19–21). At least four examples within the history of the early years of the church show clearly what happens when Christianity confronts magick.(Acts 8:9–24, 13:4–12, 16:16–24, 19:13–20).

Spiritism has become a popular occult practice, because people are intrigued by the the prospect of making contact with the spirits of the dead. In 1 Samuel 28, King Saul sought advice from the dead prophet Samuel through a witch who lived in a city called Endor.

The tantalizing question is, Can people really contact the spirits of the dead? Jesus called Lazarus and two others back from the dead. Why should we not at least be able to talk to them?

While in 1 Samuel 28 it seems unclear as to whether Saul actually spoke with Samuel, in other passages of the Bible God clearly condemned even the attempt at such practices. Although Saul had forbidden these practices, in desperation he later relented and personally accepted assistance from a spiritistic medium.

God makes it clear that this practice, called necromancy, is contrary to His will and it cannot provide valid information, because Satan, its author, is a father of lies (John 8:44). In this case, simply to be neutral is not enough (Matt. 12:30). We are to stand up to Satan and his wily ways. "Resist the devil and he will flee from you" (James 4:7). When Saul actually got what he wanted, or what he thought he wanted, he was terrified at what he heard (1 Chron. 10:13–14). Although spiritism has been practised for years, a new dimension has been added more recently. By pretending to contact the spirits of former spiritual guides who are now deceased, many people claim the ability to help people direct their lives into the future. These trance-channelers attempt to gain a following by propounding the preposterous lie of reincarnation.

There's a New Age Dawning!

As the end of the world approaches, Satan is working frantically, seeking to gain as many followers as he can (2 Tim. 3:1). As Christians, we also recognize another sign of Satan's desire to destroy Christ's kingdom: "For the time will come when men will not put up with sound doctrine. Instead, to suit their own desires, they will gather around them a great number of teachers to say what their itching ears want to hear. They will turn their ears away from the truth and turn aside to myths" (2 Tim. 4:3–4).

As an increasing number of people are teaching other doctrines as truth, many young Christians are listening. They need to be cautioned to measure every offer of "new" truth against God's Word and warned that Satan has designs on their souls.

For example, in January 1987, millions of television viewers heard and saw Shirley MacLaine, famous dancer, singer, and actress, play herself in a miniseries. She shouted into the sea, proclaiming, "I am God . . . I am God . . . I am God." Perhaps you and members of your family were among those who watched Miss MacLaine dissolve into giggles at the end of the scene. It was not funny! Five hours and two days later, with audiences building, viewers sobered to learn the "truth" for which Miss MacLaine had gone "out on a limb." She really believes what she is saying. She honestly thinks that she is God. She really believes that she and all other people have lived hundreds of previous lives and that by learning about these former existences we can live better in the future.

She first learned about something called the *New Age* movement from a friend. This friend suggested she seek further information from a trance-channeler. Later, after trips throughout the United States, Europe, and South America, after authoring at least five books and starring in several television appearances, Miss MacLaine articulated her new-found beliefs to the world. Through repeated contacts with "spirits" of departed masters, Miss MacLaine experienced "out of body travel." This confirmed for her a hunch that she had lived many lives before. Her popularity as a singer and dancer lent credibility to what she had been saying for several years.

Although some people made light of what Miss MacLaine was saying, many concluded it was real. In April 1987 an article in *The Lutheran Witness* (p. 8) by Rev. Philip Lochhaas, Executive Director for the Commission on Organizations of The Lutheran Church—Missouri Synod, agrees that this indeed is a force for Christians to deal with. It is especially important for our young people to recognize the New Age Movement for what it is—a cheap imitation of religion. It offers no hope of forgiveness or eternal life. Instead this loosely organized movement proclaims that we are all gods. According to the movement, the only reason that we have problems in life is that we don't recognize that we are gods. We need to be transformed by altering our consciousness.

As might be expected, immediately after Miss MacLaine's TV miniseries, she and others with similar beliefs began conducting seminars across the country. One woman from the northeastern part of the United States packed auditoriums with people who had paid $2,000 each to attend her weekend meetings. She claimed that the spirit of a creature who had lived 50,000 years before was speaking through her body and mouth. She championed the same beliefs as Miss MacLaine—"We are all gods. We can only realize our full potential as we accept this fact!"

The New Age movement is actually not new. It is a hodgepodge of spirit worship, Hindu mysticism, transcendental meditation, and avant-garde psychology. While some people may shrug their shoulders or laugh it off, it definitely is a force to be reckoned with. It poses a threat to the Christian family because it seeks to provide answers to questions our young people are asking. It is our duty as parents to listen to what our young people are learning.

Some people feel that the New Age is an organized conspiracy seeking the systematic overthrow of worldwide Christianity. We must label these New Age ideas as satanic and identify them as the fakes they really are. Perhaps they are most threatening because they fit into the jiffy-solution mentality of our day. People are looking for ready-made, packaged answers. It does not tax the intellect and provides a strong and immediate answer to questions that otherwise may remain unanswered. Never mind that the answers are false and deadly!

As Christian parents, we ought to question anything that offers a quick and easy solution for the problems of people, especially youth. We ought to question teachers and organizations which freely use undefinable terms that have come to be buzzwords of the occult, such as *centering*, *visualization*, *the inner self*, and *transpersonal learning*. Many companies and schools have used these techniques, billing them as consciousness-expanding.

This is the time to ask penetrating questions of our young people who are exposed to the techniques: What world-views have been propounded, what has been said specifically or implied about the nature of God, and the solutions for the problems of the world?

When our young people find the church and traditional worship lifeless and boring, caution them that simply gravitatating toward something new can be risky. Remind them, as someone has said, that people who stand for nothing will fall for anything. Help them know what they believe about themselves and their Creator and Redeemer. Assure them of God's constant love for them.

Just for Fun

Fantasy is a part of everyone's life. Games and toys are as important for the emotional development of children as food is for their physical well-being. Some psychologists express concern, however, over the types of fantasy encouraged by toys, games and books. What are we teaching our children when we provide them with toys and stories with mythological (unicorns, dragons, castles) or futuristic (spacemen, robots) characters that deal with the supernatural? Are we condoning the occult when we give them toys that encourage occult practices (magic spells, sorcery, and incantations) and let them view cartoons and videos also dominated by fantasy and occult-honoring characters?

The argument continues: When children choose to play with toys, such as a truck or a doll, their imaginations roam freely, and the toys become an extension of their mind. When, however, children are given the toys together with a graphic description of how someone else feels they should be used, for example, in a movie or a cartoon, their imagination is limited, or rather projected, only in certain directions. Although the suggestions may be wholesome, consider this when providing toys and games for children. Certain fantasy items have always been predisposed to violence. Many are now being introduced that direct the mind to the occult.

A Sunday school teacher recently asked her class for examples of how they could help a young sibling feel more comfortable when left alone. One child suggested that they could pretend that He-Man was in the room. Another young child heard a radio evangelist talk about Jesus as the master of the universe. He protested to his mother, ''But mommy, everyone knows that Jesus isn't master of the universe, He-Man is.

Parents must ask how the extension of certain play will affect their children's concept of the supernatural. Will they confuse the magical powers of the Care-Bears with that of God? Are they able to make the distinction between make-believe and Biblical reality? Does it help to make that distinction when we pay no attention to the toys and games that shape their spiritual development? Check whether God or the magic of cartoons receives more of their time and attention! Interesting treatment of the topics of the occult and toys can be found in *Turmoil in the Toybox* by Phil Phillips (Lancaster, Pa.: Starburst Publications, 1986).

Many parents have expressed concern how teenagers fantasize when roleplaying (FRP) games such as Dungeons and Dragons. The game is played without a board and pieces, but with fictitious characters and books of rules. Public concern surfaced when a young undergraduate student at the University of Michigan mysteriously disappeared after several intense sessions of D&D. Friends speculated that his disappearance was somehow associated with his intense involvement in D&D and that he had mysteriously disappeared in the maze of corridors and passages in the game he had been playing.

When he surfaced unharmed a month later in Texas he claimed that there was no connection between his disappearance and the game. A year later, however, when he committed suicide, people began to wonder. Publicity began to mount and curiosities were aroused. People tried unsuccessfully to make some connection between his disappearance and subsequent death and his involvement in D&D and other FRP games. None could be made. Some suggested that the founders of D&D raise a monument to this young man. His death caused sales of the game to skyrocket. Curious and serious players seemed to be everywhere.

In their book *Playing with Fire*, authors James Weldon and James Bjornstad (Chicago: Moody Press, 1984) recount story after story, similar to the one mentioned above. These evangelical Christian authors condemn any game in which people pronounce curses and seek to destroy others, even if it is only make-believe. Since FRP games, of which D&D is only one, contain many practices forbidden in Scripture, the authors of this very significant book suggest that Christians steer clear of such questionable entertainment.

They isolate at least seven different occult practices used in these games that are forbidden by Scripture: occult magic and casting of spells, protective inscriptions, astral projection and soul travel, necromancy (contacting spirits of the dead), conjuring of demons, occult alignment with powers and deities, and using names of occult or magical orders. Concerned parents and their teens could on the basis of Scripture profit from a joint study of this book, *Playing with Fire*, using the main points of the book as an outline for discussion.

Parents of younger children might consider comparing the use of their children's toys against the following list of 12 forbidden practices.

1. Enchantments—influencing through use of charms and incantations, practicing magic arts (Lev. 19:26; Deut. 18:10–12; 2 Chron. 33:6; 2 Kings 17:17; Is. 47:8–11; Jer. 27:8; Dan. 1:20).
2. Witchcraft—dealing with evil spirits; use of sorcery or magic (Deut. 19:10–12; 2 Chron. 33:6; 1 Sam. 15:23; Gal. 5:11–21).
3. Sorcery—use of power gained from assistance or control of evil spirits, especially for divining (Jer. 27:9; Is. 47:9; Rev. 21:8).
4. Divination—fortune telling (Deut. 18:10–14; 2 Kings 17:17; Jer. 27:8–9; 29:8–9; Acts 16:16–24).
5. Wizardry—practicing witchcraft, sorcery (Deut. 18:11; 2 Kings 17:17; Exodus 22:18).
6. Necromancy—communicating with the dead; conjuring spirits of the dead for purposes of magically revealing future events or influencing the natural course of events (Deut. 18:11; 1 Sam. 28:1–25; Is. 8:19; 1 Chron. 10:13–14).
7. Charm—put a spell on people to affect them by magic (Deut. 18:11; Is. 19:3).
8. Star Gazing/Astrology—divining the influence of stars upon human affairs and character by their positions (Is. 47:12–15; Jer. 10:2; Dan. 1:18–20; 2:1–49; 4:1–37; 5:7–15).
9. Soothsaying—foretelling events, prophesying by a spirit other than the Holy Spirit of God (Joshua 13:22; Micah 5:12–15; Acts 16:16–18).
10. Prognostication—foretell from signs or symptoms, prophesy without the Holy Spirit, similar to soothsaying (Is. 47:12–15).
11. Observing Times—astrology (Lev. 19:26; Deut. 18:10–14; 2 Kings 21:6; 2 Chron. 33:6).
12. Magic—witchcraft, occult, magick (Deut. 18:10–12; 2 Chron. 33:6; 1 Sam. 15:29).

Some argue that these are only games and that the spells and curses are only imaginary. Consider what Jesus says in Matt. 5:28. If it is possible to commit adultery in your heart, isn't it also possible to sin by becoming involved with the occult, even if you only think about it? Ask your children, "What can we do instead?" Remember, Satan wants to devour us (1 Pet. 5:8). He would deceive us at every turn (2 Cor. 2:11). If we resist the devil, he will flee from us (James 4:7).

Yours for a Song!

The same principles hold for music—the subject of another chapter in this book. For our topic here consider how music can be helpful or destructive. David played a harp for the troubled King Saul, and the king's spirit was soothed (1 Sam. 16:23). During a concert in Altamont, Calif., in 1967, a man was clubbed to death with pool cues, fists, and chains, and then was stabbed to death five times as the audience went into a frenzy while Mick Jagger sang "Jumping Jack Flash" and "Sympathy for the Devil."

These are extreme examples, but they illustrate the effect and influence of music. Some reinforces meditation and praise of God. Other music encourages rebellion against God and authority. Some encourages the use of drugs, murder and even suicide. This is satanic.

In considering the music in your home, some of the following may be useful:

1. Lyrics and group names: Do the lyrics honor Jesus, if they purport to be Scriptural? Would they help others find Jesus as Savior? Would they be an obstacle to discovering the way to eternal life? Consider as examples such hypnotic, repetitive tunes as "Gimmie a Bullet" or the words of "Shoot to Thrill": "Shoot to thrill—way to kill / I've got my gun and I'm ready / Pull the trigger, pull it!"

2. Life-style: Get information about the life-style of the artists in question. Are their life-styles consistent with their music? What are their priorities? For example, money is an extremely important issue in rock music.

3. Goals: Although our motives are ultimately weighed by the Lord (Prov. 16:2; Matt. 7:1), our lives bear witness to our priorities (Matt. 7:15). You can never assume that an artist is neutral.

4. Graphics: Consider what message the pictures on the album or tape cover convey. Do they honor Christ or contradict what He

teaches? The cover on Led Zeppelin's album, *House of the Holy*, depicts a child sacrificed to demons.

5. Public Performances: Contrast a "Christian" rock performance with one that includes nudity and mimicking of sex acts on stage.

This is bound to generate friction in your home since music is important to many young people, especially when peers seem to support music that you question. It may be helpful to gather a number of records and talk about them with the teenagers in your home. Using the five ideas just mentioned, rate the music on a scale from 1 to 10, 10 being completely acceptable. Help your young people plan a strategy for becoming discriminating listeners and buyers of music. Music is truly a gift from God, but it can also be a tool of Satan. Be sure the music you encourage glorifies God and His Son, our Savior.

Practical Suggestions

How can you arm yourself and help your family guard against Satan's devious ways? What can you do to help those who are involved or showing an interest in the occult? George A. Mather and Larry Nichols list the following points in an article, "Doorways to the Demonic," in the October 1987 *Lutheran Witness* (pp. 3–5):

1. Don't be afraid to share the Gospel of Christ with occultists. God's Word is sharper than any two-edged sword and is far more powerful than anything Satan can throw at us (1 John 4:4).

2. Pray for people who were interested in the occult and have become followers of Jesus. Receive them as fellow members of the body of Christ. Pray for them and offer them support. As you can imagine, Satan won't give up without a fight.

3. Do not attempt to play armchair psychologist. Direct these people to Christian psychologists and counselors. There is both a spiritual and a psychological dimension to illness!

4. Become informed about Satan and his tricks by studying the Bible. It is easy to lose your spiritual balance and become either too secure or too frightened about the possibilities Satan has available to him. Keep your eyes on Jesus and His Word. It is important to gain information from Christian rather than occult sources. Satan,

with all his tricks, will try to convince you either that he is very attractive, or no threat at all.

In seeking information about the occult, these organizations will help you:

The Commission on Organizations of The Lutheran Church—Missouri Synod, Rev. Philip Lochhaas, Executive Director, 1333 South Kirkwood Road, Saint Louis, MO, 63122-7295, 314/965-9000.

Christian Research Institute, P.O. Box 500, San Juan Capistrano, CA 92693, 714/855-9926.

Both organizations offer tracts, tapes, and information about occult activities in the United States and Canada today.

In addition to the books mentioned previously mentioned, the following may be interesting, informative and, above all, Christ-honoring:

Groothuis, Douglas R. *Unmasking the New Age.* Downers Grove: Inter-Varsity, 1986.

Lindsay, Hal. *Satan Is Alive and Well on Planet Earth.*

Grand Rapids: Zondervan, 1972.

Smith, F. LaGard. *Out on a Broken Limb.* Irvine, Calif.: Harvest House, 1986.

Wanke, Michael. *The Satan Seller.* Plainfield, N.J.: Logos International, 1972.

In Conclusion

The war against Satan is real. As you discover all the military terminology that is used in the Bible, it should be clear that Satan has squared off against Christ and all who are called by His name. The fight of faith is called good (2 Tim. 4:7). Faith is compared to a suit of armor designed to protect us (Eph. 6:11). Satan's attacks are described as fiery arrows (6:16). Even the word *gospel* was originally a technical term for the person who in warfare was dispatched to announce a victory.

Of all the weaponry that Christians possess (Eph. 6:10–17), only one piece is offensive. All the rest are meant to defend us. Only with the Word of God, the Bible (6:17), can we stand against

Satan and then only because it is Christ's Word. We are to wield it as if it were a sword; it is called the *sword of the Spirit* (6:17).

If you have trouble believing that the occult is as dangerous as described, study God's Word carefully. Surprisingly, much of Christ's own earthly ministry was in some way spent in battle with Satan. Do you dare assume that Satan won't also attack you? This is why Christ came into the world in the first place, to destroy the devil's work (1 John 3:8).

Remember the warning of C. S. Lewis. There are two opposite errors which people may fall into regarding Satan. Some foolishly doubt his existence or at least feel that he is harmless and fall easily into his traps. The other danger is to become so intense in our fear of the devil that we become overly frightened and forget Christ's victory that is ours through His shed blood.

Cling to God's Word. " You dear children are from God and have overcome them [evil spirits] because the one who is in you is greater than the one who is in the world" (1 John 4:4). Remember that "having disarmed the powers and authorities, he [Christ] made a public spectacle of them, triumphing over them by the cross" (Colossians 2:15).

Points to Remember

1. The occult stresses powers which are not of God.
2. The occult offers immediate answers to questions and problems.
3. Satan can use astrology and other forms of looking at the future to cause us to doubt our own future under God.
4. Recognize that in spite of the support of famous people, movements such as the New Age are cheap imitations of religion and offer no hope of forgiveness or eternal life.
5. Be aware of what you are teaching when providing toys and stories that deal with supernatural and occult powers.
6. Consider the 12 forbidden practices when allowing certain toys, games, music, movies, and even television programs.
7. Do not be afraid to share the Gospel with those involved in the occult.
8. Remember that God's power in Christ is supreme. We are powerful when we proclaim Him!

Peacemaking on the Family Front

Jan Case

*W*e've all heard the expression "Talk is cheap," but sometimes talk *isn't* so cheap. Sometimes talk is risky, demanding, or threatening. While conversations about the weather, sports, or politics may flow naturally and spontaneously between parents and their children, some subjects are not so easy to discuss.

The topic of this chapter is one of those "other" subjects—family disruption, a topic often difficult for adults to discuss among themselves, much less with their children. As husbands, wives, or single parents, we may be willing to acknowledge periodic disruption in our family; yet, talking about the disruption is often another matter. A husband may bury himself in work or with friends. A wife may do the same. The entire family may be aware of family tension as it gathers at the supper table, but who will raise the subject this time? Who will confront the concerns? Who will talk about the "dinosaur" everyone may acknowledge, yet everyone avoids?

What are your feelings as you begin this chapter? Is family disruption a difficult topic for you to discuss with your teen? Why?

The Tough Teen Years

No parent of a teen has escaped tears of wonder, frustration, and pain caused by a seemingly uncaring child. And no teen fails to cry out because his or her parents cannot seem to "understand." Ted Schroeder, a well-known writer of teen materials, puts it this way in *Let's Look at This the Right Way* (CPH, 1985): "If being a parent is like putting together a Christmas toy without instructions, then being the parent of a teen is like building the toy, the crate that it came in, and the truck that delivered it—all in the dark without any tools. Nothing in our lives is as challenging, confusing, and difficult as successfully nurturing a child through the years 12 to 18. And for all its problems, we find ourselves remarkably unready for the task. We have seen other people raise teens with varying degrees of success. We may even recall our own parents' attempts to bring it off. But we likely have had no courses in teen guidance, learned no rules about dealing with the changing young person, gained no set of instructions about how to make it come out right" (p. 11).

It sounds rather dismal, doesn't it? As if to complicate matters further, there are those issues which arise in every family from time to time: Tensions caused by unemployment, marital disharmony, long-term illness, an aging grandparent, or alcoholism, just for starters.

How can we talk to our teens about family disruption? How much should we tell them? Should we share our imperfections? Should we shelter them from those adult-sized problems? Should we prepare them for their own adult years? If so, how?

No time is ideal in the life of the child to experience family disruption. The challenging adolescent years are certainly no exception to that. In many respects parents of teens seem to be caught between the proverbial rock and the hard place.

Ralph Turner, a noted family therapist, describes those years in *Family Interaction* (New York: John Wiley and Sons, 1970):

"Just at the time when the adolescent is questioning the goals that society offers him and seeks guidance and assurance in making crucial choices and commitments, his parents have typically reached the stage of reassessment, doubt, and sometimes despair regarding the goals that have shaped their lives in the two or three decades since they made their own adolescent choices. Society grants little recognition to these problems. The adolescent's plea for sympathy and understanding is legitimized; the adult dares not plead for similar understanding, lest his plea destroy whatever remnant of respect continues to hold his offspring to him and lest the community write him off as a failure" (p. 397).

That does sound dismal, doesn't it? What a challenge! Perhaps we parents of teens *are* caught between a rock and a hard place.

Get a piece of paper. In one column list the major issues that face your teenager. In a second column list the major issues that face you, the parent of a teen. Why does the phrase, "the tough teen years," fittingly apply to both your teenager and you?

Popular opinion notwithstanding, teens *are* in touch with their families, and intimately so. Teens don't live in a vacuum and are not blind to what is going on around them. Teens may seem muddled, confused, disorganized, even indifferent. But teens are in touch with their families and the messages the family conveys.

Research confirms the tremendous impact of family environment upon the volatile teenager. For example, research shows that teens are acutely sensitive to the level of regard their parents have for one another. A highly distraught relationship between a mother and a father is a contributing factor to their teen's own perception of his or her worth. Violent behavior in the home has been found to be a contributing factor to later violence in the teen's own relationships. Unresolved disruption in the home is a contributing factor to teenage truancy, drug abuse, suicide, and low self-esteem.

Researchers are not the only ones who testify to the vital impact of the home upon the teen. Teens speak for themselves. *Good News about Kids*, a pamphlet produced by the Board for Youth Services of the Lutheran Church Missouri Synod, 1984, significantly and surprisingly reports results of a survey showing that parent-child relationships are more influential than generally believed. Contrary to public opinion, peers, so often cited as a negative factor, do not dominate the young person's life. In this study, though the strength of the relationship among peers increases with each grade, it was found that at no age level did peers exert more influence on the adolescent than did parents. In fact, parents were the number one choice by these teens in times of trouble, crisis, or problems.

In an earlier study, *Five Cries of Youth*, by Merton P. Strommen (New York: Harper & Row, 1974), church youth identified among their concerns: (1) The cry of self-hatred. Self-esteem, "feeling good about oneself and one's family," is a vital element in a young person's life. When it is lacking, alienating and self-destructive types of behavior appear. When it is present, life takes on excitement and purpose. (2) The cry of psychological orphans. The most poignant cry is the sob of despair or shame or sheer frustration among youths living in atmospheres of parental hatred and distrust and disappointment in the family unit.

A subsequent study, *Five Cries of Parents,* names the wants of parents of adolescents as the cry for understanding; the cry for close family; the cry for moral behavior; the cry for shared faith; and the cry for outside help. What relationship do you see between the cries of youth and the cries of parents? How do your cries or the cries of your teen compare with these research findings?

The cries of teens demonstrate the powerful influence of the family environment. Likewise, parents cry for better relations and understanding with their teenagers. Teens do not mature apart from their families. On the contrary, teen growth is largely dependent upon the family environment. While continuous disruption in the family can inhibit such growth, positive resolution of crises can serve as a catalyst for growth.

Family Disruption, Let's Look at It This Way

Family represents an arena in which people meet. Disagreements or disruptions regularly arise that test the stability of the family and the emotional maturity of its members.

One author described the many causes of family disruption: "A crisis may suddenly and unexpectedly strike into a family. The sudden death of a parent or a child, the unexpected loss of the husband's job, the destruction of property by fire or storm, are experiences which create emotional strains and frequently have disastrous effects . . . Likewise, infidelity of a mate or delinquency of a child may cause personal disorganizations often beyond repair" (Oscar E. Feucht, *Helping Families through the Church*, CPH, 1970).

Consider these situations:

- Last month Grandfather Mueller died quite suddenly. Grandmother, who has Alzheimer's disease, has now moved into our home. We are at a loss as to what to do or what to say. It seems to be getting worse every day.
- Dad always enjoyed his work. He took pride in his job. Dad is now laid off indefinitely.
- It seems Mom and Dad are always fighting. If it's not one thing, it's another. Last week it was money; today, who knows what?
- It's not that people shouldn't drink at all, but I'm getting worried about my wife. She doesn't seem to be her old self anymore. She seems distant and uncaring. I wonder if the children have noticed anything, especially the oldest who is nearly 16.
- The doctors say he'll eventually get better. They say it's just taking a long time to recover from the chemotherapy. I'm afraid these trying times are starting to take their toll on the whole family.
- Teenagers must be crazy! There's just no pleasing them. The louder I yell, the worse it seems to get. I haven't talked to my teen in weeks. What's going on?

Not all crises have discouraging consequences for family life. The death of a husband and father may knit the survivors into a closer, more fully integrated group. The widowed mother and her children may form a stronger bond in order to cope.

Unfortunately, not all critical situations in family life have wholesome outcomes. In many instances the results are devastating. Individuals may go to pieces physically and mentally. Some Christians may even lose their spiritual balance.

In whatever form they appear, family crises are the result of sin. All people alike are victims of sin's consequences—sickness, death, and sorrow. People's sinful, perverted hearts cause them to stray from God's Word, bringing shame and unbearable grief on those nearest them.

Family disruption generates real hurts and needs for both teens and parents exposing problems that will often accuse us. Ted Schroeder in *Let's Look at This the Right Way* wrote: "These basic hurts, needs, and conflicts will not simply go away in time or be resolved by good intentions and hard work. They will need the power and presence that God offers by His Spirit in our Savior Jesus Christ. In Him we have reason to hope even in the face of what may seem unsolvable problems and impossible conflicts" (p. 12).

Reread that last quote. Summarize it in your own words. How does that message comfort you as a parent of a teen?

To Talk or Not to Talk—That Is the Question!

- "My mother and father never argued in front of me, so I don't think we should argue in front of our children either."
- "What they don't know won't hurt them. They don't need to know about these things."
- "If I admit there's a problem, my children won't think I'm perfect anymore."
- "If I just ignore it, maybe it will go away."

Do those comments sound familiar? They are among the most common ideas that race through a parent's mind when there is disruption in the family.

The first comment reflects a very idealistic approach. The "My parents never did, and we shouldn't either" comment sounds like an excuse. The second comment, "What they don't know won't hurt them," is fallacious. The fact is that children often *do* know more than you realize, especially teenage children. The tension at the supper table, the silent treatment a husband gives his wife, the slamming of doors, and the heated, late-night disagreements are impossible to conceal. The third comment, "They won't think I'm perfect anymore," summarizes unrealistic expectations. It reminds us of the tremendous burden of guilt which parents often impose upon themselves. The fourth comment, "Ignore it," is simply avoidance, often a futile attempt to sweep it under the rug, hoping the concern will somehow mend itself.

Those four attitudes each contain a degree of fact and fiction. The truth lies somewhere between. Family conflicts can actually teach children how to handle—and survive—disruption. In general, healthy confrontation is better than avoidance at all costs. Children sense strong feelings and conflicts through even the most carefully maintained mask. To deny feelings altogether, or to express them only when the children are absent, can be as damaging as displaying them in excessive, uncontrolled warfare. From the former, children learn that negative feelings are either forbidden or their expression is relegated to the closet. From the latter, they learn that such feelings are dangerous because they can be neither redirected or controlled.

Which of the four statements most closely describes your own feelings? Which describes your parents' approach to such matters? The approach of the parents of your spouse? Acknowledging and resolving family disruption can be instructive for the entire family. Conflict can be productive. Productive conflict starts with a disagreement and ends with people reaching some kind of resolution. Children need to see that conflicts are part of life and can be worked out eventually. In other words, fighting can be good, as long as you know how to be productive about it. If people never grew or changed, if they married people just like themselves, or if they were perfect, they wouldn't need to fight. But positive fighting, the acknowledgment of disruption and the resolution of conflict can enhance growth in parents and teens alike.

From witnessing everyday arguments between parents, for example, children can learn that people can love each other and still get angry, argue about something, resolve the issue, and get over it. This is an important lesson to learn about how to live in a close relationship. It also reassures children about the strength of a relationship that can withstand anger and conflict. This is why it is so important for children to see the resolution of the argument. If parents continually begin fights in front of the children and then withdraw to finish the fight, the children may imagine that things are worse than they are.

Children need assurance that they are not the sole cause of every family disruption, a common fantasy among children. Failure to acknowledge disruption can be harmful to a child. For example, when a child feels he does not know what has actually happened to break up his parents' marriage, he is apt to be more disturbed than he would be if he were taken into their confidence. He may feel isolated and fill the gap with what he imagines. Many times what he imagines has to do with himself.

Talking to teens implies a willingness to listen to their feelings and apprehensions. "To talk or not to talk?" often needs to be balanced with "To listen or not to listen?" "With the assurance that we are forgiven for whatever part we have in creating the confrontations that happen between ourselves and our teens, with the hope that Christ brings for help in the most difficult of human dilemmas, we have the courage to look closely at our dealings with our children—so that we might put away the hurts and mistakes of the past and find new ways to show love, to share forgiveness, and to build one another up by the power of the Spirit." (*Let's Look at This the Right Way*, p. 12.)

Reread that quote again. How does it relate to the concern, "To talk or not to talk?" What characterizes Christian conversation?

Communication—the "How To"

Talking with your teen needs to be two-way; it's talking and listening; it's conversation. You send messages (you speak) and you also receive messages (you listen). Positive conversation requires the willingness and the skill to express yourself to your child. Positive conversation also requires the willingness and the skill to listen to your teen.

Parents can be genuine in expressing their emotions to children without attacking their character or arousing hostility. One way is to give "I" messages rather than "you" messages. "I" messages express your personal feelings, while "you" messages tend to accuse the child of being bad.

For instance, "I don't like having my sleeve pulled" would probably elicit more cooperation from a young child than "Stop being such a pest!" Talk about what you're feeling, not what's wrong with the other person. As Earl Gaulke writes in *You Can Have a Family Where Everyone Wins*, "Law-oriented power statements may well lead your child to be defensive or to have feelings of being put down." Here are some additional examples: "How would you like it if I did that to you?" (teaching); "Hey, dummy, how about turning the TV up a little so all of us can go deaf?"

(name-calling); "Are you trying to get even with me for something that's bugging you?" (interpreting).

By contrast, telling your child how you feel with a nonblaming description of the behavior that is interfering with your needs is a more positive way to communicate. It is (1) non-judgmental, (2) conveys your trust in him or her as a person who is a child of God and is empowered by God's Spirit, (3) forces him or her to regard your need willingly, out of love, and (4) facilitates your child's growth in the new life in Christ, the life which relates constructively and lovingly to others.

Describe your style of communication with your teen. Ask your teen to do the same. How do your answers compare?

Besides speaking, the art of listening is also crucial to good parent-teen communication. In *The Five Cries of Parents*, Merton Strommen lists three types of listening mistakes: "Listening with half an ear" (attending to other matters and not giving your adolescent the benefit of your entire attention); "Yes, but" listening (quickly launching into the advice before you even heard your teen); and "I can top that" listening (shifting the attention to yourself and not responding to the feelings the other person has expressed).

Listening with the heart is a basic requirement for understanding children or people of any age. Listening is the only way we as parents can come to understand the thoughts, concerns, and feelings of our children, especially those unique to our teens.

Strommen (pp. 65–67) lists three suggestions for effective listening:

"Guide 1—Listen in ways that encourage expression of feelings. Adolescence is a time of bewildering emotions and intense new feelings. This includes sexual desires, fantasies, grandiose ambitions, dreams, anger at being treated like a child, and strange feelings about bodily changes. Not until an adolescent identifies those feelings with words will he or she begin to handle them in a rational, mature way."

"Guideline 2—Listen to discover the adolescent's perspective. This means listening to discover where your adolescent is 'coming from.' It means trying to understand how your child views life. It means trying to view a situation through the eyes of your adolescent. It doesn't mean that at this point we stop being parents. But it does mean that we make a deliberate attempt to know the inner life and feelings of our child. Such knowledge is a parent's best guide for determining how best to respond."

"**Guideline 3**—Approach each conversation with a sense of hope. The adolescent may be fearful and deeply troubled. Trapped by peer pressure, he or she may become involved in problems created by drugs or alcohol abuse, sexual activity, or vandalism. It is important that. . . there (be) hope, regardless of the situation. . . . Adolescents, sensing this confidence in them, will receive it as good news of the highest order." Ultimately, confidence in God gives a sense of hope to the conversations we have with our children.

How do you stack up with these pointers? Which others would you add?

Talking with our teens is just that: it's talking *with*, not talking *down to*, or talking *around*, or talking *against* teens. Those polished skills don't magically appear for us when our children become teens. They require years of practice. They begin early in life as we set the foundation for later conversations with our children. The solid basics of communication aren't merely pulled out of storage and hurriedly applied when there is an impending crisis. Willingness to express our feelings and listen attentively to our children are day-to-day skills, to be used in times of satisfaction, not just dissatisfaction.

Building on the Basics

Talking with Your Teen about Family Disruption

The groundwork for good communication between parent and child begins in the early years. Parents who push aside their small children with "I'm busy" find that the time cannot be recaptured in teenage years. The busyness does not decrease over the years. If a parent does not have time for very young children, it will be difficult to find time during the teen years as well. In the same way, parents who listen to the language of a child's behavior in the preschool years will also be able to "hear" the actions of their adolescents—their joys and sorrows, their happiness with regard to family life, and their uneasiness with family disruption.

Good listening and talking skills will equip you to talk with your teen in a natural way. The willingness for you to "level" and to "listen" are the skills which will guide you as you talk about career dreams, school work, dating, and even family disruption. An open system of communication will be of tremendous value as you face family disruption and consider what to say, when to say it, and how to say it.

Now let's build on the basics. The decision to talk or not to talk about family disruption is often a difficult one to make. There are no glib answers. You will find here no simple solutions. However, if good communication skills are practiced in the family, discussions about this troublesome topic can be more meaningful for all.

If you practice good listening skills you will more readily grasp the strain disruption places on a teen. If you display a willingness to listen to your child, the "how to" and the "when to" will come much easier. Likewise, if you have been willing to share your feelings on other subjects of importance to you, your feelings concerning disruption will more likely be easier to share.

Why are good communication skills necessary for talking to your teen about family disruption? How can good communication skills guide you when you face disruption in your family?

Teens need assurance that they are not the only cause of family disruption. To make sure that you are not unwittingly adding fuel to the fire, parents should be honest and forthright. But how honest? How forthright? How much is enough? How much is not quite enough?

To a great extent the answers depend upon your teen's questions, feelings, and needs. The disadvantages of either extreme are easy to identify. On the one hand, failure to acknowledge their questions altogether is detrimental. On the other hand, putting everything on the table can be just as detrimental. For instance, in the case of marital disruption, you wouldn't want your teen to assume the role of a peacemaker between yourself and your spouse or express opinions about who is right and who is wrong. This may seem relatively harmless and even cute at the time, but if it becomes a habit, it can induce a sense of responsibility for parents' actions that is too great a burden for a child as well as for a teen.

Here is one list of potential dos and don'ts concerning parental conflicts, one cause of family disruption.

DO

- Let children observe normal arguments about everyday things.
- Let children see the end of an argument, or tell them that the fight was resolved.
- Assure children that it is not their fault that you are fighting. Be aware of what information children are getting from an argument.
- Call a family conference if the issues legitimately concern the children.
- Reassure children if they have reason to fear that fighting may lead to divorce.
- Practice the rules for "good" fighting.

DON'T

- Fight about money problems or relatives in front of children.
- Fight about sex or intimate marital problems in front of children.
- Fight about child-rearing decisions in front of children.
- Let children see you and your spouse repeatedly lose control in fights.
- Use children as referees or spectators in parental arguments.
- Let children take sides in your arguments.
- Use verbal abuse or physical violence.

The suggestions readily apply to many types of family disruption. How families deal with disruption is critical to healthy relationships in the home. It's been said that there are three basic ways to handle anger: inflict it, suppress it, or deal with it and work through the problem at hand. That also holds true for the discussion of major family disruption. The third option, of course, is desirable. That requires good message-sending and good message-receiving skills.

Consider These Suggestions

Teens live in a fuzzy territory between childhood and adulthood. In crises, they may react with rapid fluctuations between childlike and adult behavior, or they may choose to act consistently either as adults or as children. Parents may contribute unwittingly to one or the other behavior by responding more readily to it, taking for granted that the youngster is "still a child" (and therefore doesn't understand) or "already a young adult" (and therefore a peer). A childlike stance may, among other possibilities, be an expression of dependency and a plea to restore harmony for the "baby's sake"; and an adultlike facade may, as one possibility, be an attempt to achieve an alliance with one parent, or it could be an attempt to indulge a curiosity about parents' private lives. In periods of crisis, parents should at various moments "read" their child to understand his or her attitude, and thus avoid forgetting the "child" when the youngster is behaving as an adult, or avoid the "adult" when the teen acts like a child.

The boundaries must also be clear. Some things belong to the couple's realm and should not be shared with the teen, regardless of the parents' temptation to find an ally in him or her. A clear boundary that preserves the privacy of the details of parental conflict is as wise as keeping the bedroom door closed when having sex, though not refraining from demonstrating affection and tenderness in the presence of the children.

So two points of caution are in order: First, when adults decide to inform children about touchy issues, they may betray their anxiety by going overboard, overinforming beyond the need for the child's age. Second, if the teen starts to cry or express similar strong emotions, the parent, because of guilt, may try to pacify with promises, complaints, or rationalizations, rather than offering the most useful behavior of all, just being receptive as well as respectful of the outpouring of emotion. (Adapted from *The Parents' Guide to Teenagers* [New York: Macmillan, 1981].)

Summarize these last three paragraphs in your own words. Which ideas are most helpful for you right now?

It is important for adolescents and their parents to share problems, experiences, and ideas so they can come to a better understanding of each other. If the family is to be a unit in which each individual is at ease and trusts the other, this is necessary. However, there are obvious limits to this sharing. There is a touchy demarcation line that each family must determine for itself. A respect for privacy is as important to family harmony as is the feeling that in moments of disruption the teen can depend on his or her parents.

"I'm Sorry"

The apology plays an important role as you talk to your teen about family disruption. Psychologists, psychiatrists, family counselors, and mental-health practitioners agree that a sincere apology from a parent that is specific and simple can have a lifelong effect upon a child. That's a vital truth for Christian parents as well.

When you apologize (with words or actions, or both) you teach your child that a person doesn't have to be right all the time. All people, though redeemed by Christ, are still sinners who make mistakes. The teen learns that it's all right even for the parent to make a mistake and to admit it. By hearing parents apologize, children are taught that they, too, can make mistakes, admit them, and be forgiven.

That's an important truth when we talk with our teens about family disruption. In fact, when you let your child know that it is you who are wrong, you bolster rather than diminish your child's confidence in others and himself. The proverbial "communication gap" is not created suddenly when a child approaches adolescence. Rather, it is developed over years of refusal to open up and express feelings to children. An apology can be the start of a healthy conversation about how to make things better between parent and child.

Forgiveness plays a critical role in Christian family relationships. How would you describe the role forgiveness plays in your family?

In the context of forgiveness, Harold Hazelip (*Happiness in the Home* [Grand Rapids: Baker Books, 1985]) offers these concise steps when parents face disruption in the family: First, face the crisis. In the long run, the world of fantasy and denial is worse than reality. Refusing to acknowledge what has happened will only complicate the problem. The healthy response is to admit the truth and do what must be done to minimize the ill effects. Second, feel your hurt. All failures involve loss, and loss always brings grief, which can be delayed, but cannot be avoided. Third, talk to someone. Find someone you trust who will care enough to listen. Just talking about it can help more than you imagine. Fourth, seek help. Sometimes professional help is most appropriate and helpful. Fifth, accept your limits. One of the hardest realities to face is the awareness that the only person you can change or control is yourself. You can, however, manage yourself in such a way that others will be influenced to manage themselves differently. Finally, keep in touch with your support group. Crisis time is no time to be alone. We all need people, especially when the family unit is in trouble. Maintain contact with friends, neighbors, and church.

Some Concluding Thoughts

Sin is the force which disrupts families. It rears its head in many ways. It separates people from one another and people from their God. In Christ, we possess the wherewithal to confront those disruptive forces in our families. Through His Spirit we are guided to talk about disruption. Through His Spirit we learn caring and listening skills as we bring the Gospel. While no family is entirely free of disruption, conflict does offer an opportunity to apply those skills to our most cherished relationships.

Throughout the Scriptures we marvel over God's unmerited love for us and then what this means for daily living. That is the faith we teach in formal ways, through structured times like daily family devotions, evening prayer, regular attendance with the larger family of God in worship services, and church schools. But that is also the faith we impart through informal daily conversation. We share "what Jesus means to me" in those teachable moments. Those opportune moments also occur in the midst of, or in the wake of, family disruption.

What contributes most to family disruption? What variables are most frequently associated with a tense emotional climate? Strommen, in *The Five Cries of Youth*, concluded that the one factor that most strongly predicts family disunity is the simple statement "My father and mother do not get along. This bothers me." Ranking second in predictive power is parental distrust. Unless the parents are helped to make peace with each other and learn what it means to trust, children will suffer, even at 18 years of age.

In spite of facts learned and advice heard, parenting is in the final analysis a matter of coping, hoping, and growing. There is no end to our challenges. There are few easy solutions. As parents we are continually reacting to what is happening and seldom able to plan systematically and carry out those plans. On the other hand, offering our love together with the knowledge that the body of Christ has been blessed by the presence of our children is enriching indeed.

Recognizing that there will be problems and that we cannot expect to handle them by ourselves with quick and easy dispatch are first steps to good parenting. Retaining hope through all is a further step. Of course, that is the essence of our Christian faith. We live in constantly renewed hope. As parents, living in hope means that we reaffirm God's care for parents as well as for children.

Perhaps the place of greatest challenge to mutual ministry is in our homes. The very closeness that makes us a family can cause disruption but, even more seriously, it can cause us to look past one another, to focus on our own needs and to take one another for granted. As parents of teens who are living at a particularly complex and confusing time of their lives, we need to seek God's help and the support of one another, even the support of our teens.

Teens can offer forgiveness, understanding, and love when parents fail to be what they would like to be, or what the teen would like them to be. The principal identifying mark of the Christian home is not perfection but love that shows itself in forgiveness. "With the assurance that we are forgiven for whatever part we have in creating the confrontations that happen in a family, with the hope that Christ brings for help in the most difficult of human dilemmas, we have the courage to look closely at our dealings with our children and *talk*—that we might put away the hurts and mistakes of the past and find new ways to build one another up in His power" (paraphrased from *Let's Look at This the Right Way*, p. 12).

Points to Remember

1. Teens are not blind to what is going on around them.
2. Teens are highly sensitive to the level of regard parents have for one another.
3. The power and presence that God offers by His Spirit in our Savior Jesus Christ is what gives hope in what may seem to be unsolvable problems and conflicts.
4. Family conflict can actually teach children how to handle and

survive disruption. Healthy confrontation is better than avoidance at all costs.
5. Talking to teens must also include a willingness to listen to their feelings and apprehensions.
6. An open communication system is of tremendous value when facing family disruption.
7. A balance needs to be maintained between respect for privacy and the sharing of issues and problems.
8. Ultimately, who we are in Jesus Christ will govern all of our relationships with one another.